# BIG IT UP

Designs by
Martin Storey • Carol Meldrum • Leah Sutton
Lucinda Guy • Antoni & Alison • Sarah Hatton
Lisa Richardson • Theresa Venning • Jennie Atkinson

**Nothing** front & back by Antoni & Alison

**Afghan** by Martin Storey

*This page* **Elsa** by Jennie Atkinson
*Opposite* **Erin** by Theresa Venning

*This page* **Yulah** by Leah Sutton
*Opposite* **Laura** by Sarah Hatton

*This page* **Daisy** by Theresa Venning
*Opposite* **Berber Bag** by Martin Storey

**Lotta** by Lucinda Guy

*This page* **Ulla** *Opposite* **Lilla** both by Lucinda Guy

Ellie by Lucinda Guy

# Index

# LOCKI

## LEAH SUTTON

## YARN

|  | XS | S | M | L | XL |  |
|---|---|---|---|---|---|---|
| To fit bust | 81 | 86 | 91 | 97 | 102 | cm |
|  | 32 | 34 | 36 | 38 | 40 | in |

**Rowan Big Wool Tuft and Big Wool**
A Tuft Night Sky 060

|  | 5 | 6 | 6 | 7 | 7 | x 50gm |
|---|---|---|---|---|---|---|

B Big Glamour 036

|  |  | 1 | 2 | 2 | 2 | 3 | x 100gm |
|---|---|---|---|---|---|---|---|

## NEEDLES

1 pair 10mm (no 000) (US 15) needles
1 pair 12mm (US 17) needles

## FASTENING – 1 kilt pin

## TENSION

8 sts and 12 rows to 10 cm measured over
stocking stitch using 12mm (US 17) needles.

## BACK

Using 12mm (US 17) needles and yarn A cast
on 30 [32: 34: 36: 38] sts.
**Row 1 (RS):** K1, ★K2tog, yfwd, rep from ★
to last st, K1.
**Row 2:** Purl.
**Row 3:** Inc in first st, ★yfwd, K2tog tbl, rep
from ★ to last st, inc in last st.
**Row 4:** Purl.
These 4 rows form patt and start shaping.
Cont in patt, inc 1 st at each end of next and
foll 14 alt rows, taking inc sts into patt.
62 [64: 66: 68: 70] sts.
Work 15 rows, ending with RS facing for next
row. (Back should meas 40 cm.)

Break yarn, leaving a long end of approx
150 cm, and leave sts on a holder.

## LEFT FRONT

Using 12mm (US 17) needles and yarn A cast
on 15 [16: 17: 18: 19] sts.
**Row 1 (RS):** K1, ★K2tog, yfwd, rep from ★
to last 2 [1: 2: 1: 2] sts, K2 [1: 2: 1: 2].
**Row 2:** Purl.
**Row 3:** Inc in first st, ★yfwd, K2tog tbl, rep
from ★ to last 2 [1: 2: 1: 2] sts, K2 [1: 2: 1: 2].
**Row 4:** Purl.
These 4 rows form patt.
Cont in patt, inc 1 st at beg (side edge) of next
and foll 10 alt rows, taking inc sts into patt.
27 [28: 29: 30: 31] sts.
Work 1 row, ending with RS facing for next
row.
**Shape front edge**
Keeping patt correct, inc 1 st at end (front
opening edge) of next and foll 4th row, then
on foll 4 alt rows **and at same time** inc 1 st
at beg (side edge) of next and foll 3 alt rows.
37 [38: 39: 40: 41] sts.
Work 1 row, ending with RS facing for next
row.
**Shape neck**
**Next row (RS):** Patt 29 [30: 31: 32: 33] sts
and turn, leaving rem 8 sts on a holder.
Dec 1 st at neck edge of next 6 rows.
23 [24: 25: 26: 27] sts.
Work 1 row, ending with RS facing for
next row.
**Join shoulder**
Holding WS of back against WS of left front,

cast off sts of left front tog with first 23 [24:
25: 26: 27] sts of back. (Cast off edge will show
on RS.)

## RIGHT FRONT

Using 12mm (US 17) needles and yarn A cast
on 5 [6: 7: 8: 9] sts.
**Row 1 (RS):** K0 [1: 0: 1: 0], ★K2tog, yfwd,
rep from ★ to last st, K1.
**Row 2:** Purl.
**Row 3:** K0 [1: 0: 1: 0], ★yfwd, K2tog tbl, rep
from ★ to last st, inc in last st.
**Row 4:** Purl.
These 4 rows form patt and start shaping.
Cont in patt, inc 1 st at beg (front opening
edge) of next and foll 3 alt rows, then at same
edge on foll 5 rows **and at same time** inc
1 st at end (side edge) of next and foll 5 alt
rows, ending with RS facing for next row and
taking inc sts into patt.
21 [22: 23: 24: 25] sts.
Cast on 3 sts at beg and inc 1 st at end of next
row. 25 [26: 27: 28: 29] sts.
Inc 1 st at end (side edge) **only** of 2nd and foll
7 alt rows. 33 [34: 35: 36: 37] sts.
Work 7 rows, ending with RS facing for next
row.
**Shape neck**
**Next row (RS):** Patt 4 sts and slip these sts
onto a holder, patt to end.
29 [30: 31: 32: 33] sts.
Dec 1 st at neck edge of next 6 rows.
23 [24: 25: 26: 27] sts.
Work 1 row, ending with RS facing for
next row.

### Join shoulder

Break yarn.

Holding WS of back against WS of right front and using length of yarn left with back (so starting cast-off at outer side edge), cast off sts of right front tog with first 23 [24: 25: 26: 27] sts of back. (There should be 16 sts of back left on holder at centre back neck.)

### MAKING UP

Press as described on the information page.

### Neckband

With RS facing, using 10mm (US 15) needles and yarn B, slip 4 sts from right front holder onto right needle, rejoin yarn and pick up and knit 7 sts up right side of neck, K rem 16 sts from back holder, pick up and knit 7 sts down left side of neck, then K 8 sts from left front holder. 42 sts.

Work in g st for 2 rows, ending with **WS** facing for next row.

Cast off knitwise (on **WS**).

### Disk

Using 10mm (US 15) needles and yarn B cast on 140 sts.

Cast off knitwise (on **WS**).

See information page for finishing instructions. Coil disk strip up to form a disk and sew in place. Sew disk to right front as in photograph. Fasten neck with kilt pin.

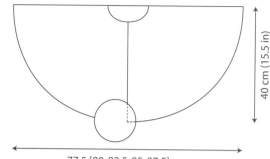

40 cm (15.5 in)

77.5 [80: 82.5: 85: 87.5] cm
(30.5 [31.5: 32.5: 33.5: 34.5] in)

No. 2

# PETUNA

## LISA RICHARDSON

### YARN

**Rowan Big Wool**

1 x 100gm
(photographed in White Hot 001)

### NEEDLES

1 pair 10mm (no 000) (US 15) needles

### BUTTONS – 30 large(16 x 00369, 14 x 00378) and 30 small (16 x 00374, 14 x 00383)

### TENSION

8½ sts and 13 rows to 10 cm measured over stocking stitch using 10mm (US 15) needles.

### MITTS (both alike)

Using 10mm (US 15) needles cast on 20 sts.

**Row 1 (RS):** K1, (P2, K2) 4 times, P2, K1.

**Row 2:** P1, (K2, P2) 4 times, K2, P1.

Rep last 2 rows for 14 cm, ending with RS facing for next row.

**Next row (RS):** K2, (K2tog, K3) 3 times, K2tog, K1.

16 sts.

Beg with a P row, work in st st for 9 rows, ending with RS facing for next row.

Cast off.

### MAKING UP

Press as described on the information page. Join palm seam.

Using photograph as a guide, sew buttons onto back of wrist, attaching one small button on top of each large button and alternating colours. Fold mitt flat, so that seam runs centrally along length, and join cast-off edges at a point 3 cm in from one folded edge to divide upper opening edge for thumbhole and fingers.

No. 3

# LOTTA
## LUCINDA GUY

## YARN

|  | XS | S | M | L | XL |  |
|---|---|---|---|---|---|---|
| To fit bust | 81 | 86 | 91 | 97 | 102 | cm |
|  | 32 | 34 | 36 | 38 | 40 | in |

**Rowan Big Wool**

A  Bohemian 028

|  | 4 | 4 | 5 | 5 | 5 | x 100gm |
|---|---|---|---|---|---|---|

B  Whoosh 014

|  | 3 | 3 | 3 | 4 | 4 | x 100gm |
|---|---|---|---|---|---|---|

## NEEDLES

1 pair 10mm (no 000) (US 15) needles
1 pair 12mm (US 17) needles
Cable needle

## TENSION

12 sts and 10 rows to 10 cm measured over cable pattern, 10 sts and 9 rows to 10 cm measured over patterned stocking stitch using 12mm (US 17) needles.

## SPECIAL ABBREVIATIONS

**C6B** = slip next 3 sts onto cable needle and leave at back of work, K3, then K3 from cable needle; **C6F** = slip next 3 sts onto cable needle and leave at front of work, K3, then K3 from cable needle.

BACK and FRONT (both alike)
Using 10mm (US 15) needles and yarn A cast on 56 [58: 60: 62: 64] sts.
**Row 1 (RS):** P0 [1: 2: 3: 4], *P1, K1, (P2, K2) twice, P2, K1, P1, rep from * 3 times more, P0 [1: 2: 3: 4].
**Row 2:** K0 [1: 2: 3: 4], *K1, P1, (K2, P2) twice, K2, P1, K1, rep from * 3 times more, K0 [1: 2: 3: 4].
**Rows 3 and 4**: As rows 1 and 2.
Change to 12mm (US 17) needles.
**Row 5:** P0 [1: 2: 3: 4], (P1, K12, P1) 4 times, P0 [1: 2: 3: 4].
**Row 6:** K0 [1: 2: 3: 4], (K1, P12, K1) 4 times, K0 [1: 2: 3: 4].
**Row 7:** P0 [1: 2: 3: 4], (P1, C6B, C6F, P1) 4 times, P0 [1: 2: 3: 4].
**Row 8:** As row 6.
**Rows 9 and 10**: As rows 1 and 2.
These 10 rows form patt.
Using 12mm (US 17) needles throughout, work in patt for a further 17 rows, ending with **WS** facing for next row.
**Row 28 (WS):** P2 [3: 5: 2: 3], P2tog, *P3 [3: 4: 5: 5], P2tog, rep from * to last 2 [3: 5: 2: 3] sts, P to end.
45 [47: 51: 53: 55] sts.
Join in yarn B.
Beg and ending rows as indicated and using a combination of the **intarsia** and **fairisle** techniques as described on the information page, cont in patt from chart, which is worked entirely in st st beg with a K row, as folls:
Work chart rows 1 to 4, ending with RS facing for next row.
### Shape armholes
Keeping chart correct, cast off 3 sts at beg of next 2 rows.
39 [41: 45: 47: 49] sts.
Dec 1 st at each end of next 3 [3: 5: 5: 6] rows.
33 [35: 35: 37: 37] sts.
Cont straight until chart row 22 has been

completed, ending with RS facing for next row.
Now repeating chart rows 21 and 22 **only**, cont as folls:
Cont straight until armhole meas 22 [22: 23: 23: 24] cm, ending with RS facing for next row.
### Shape shoulders and neck
**Next row (RS):** Cast off 4 sts, patt until there are 7 sts on right needle and turn, leaving rem sts on a holder.
Work each side of neck separately.
Cast off 3 sts at beg of next row.
Cast off rem 4 sts.
With RS facing, rejoin yarns to rem sts, cast off centre 11 [13: 13: 15: 15] sts, patt to end.
Complete to match first side, reversing shapings.

## SLEEVES

Using 10mm (US 15) needles and yarn A cast on 28 [28: 30: 30: 30] sts.
**Row 1 (RS):** P0 [0: 1: 1: 1], *P1, K1, (P2, K2) twice, P2, K1, P1, rep from * once more, P0 [0: 1: 1: 1].
**Row 2:** K0 [0: 1: 1: 1], *K1, P1, (K2, P2) twice, K2, P1, K1, rep from * once more, K0 [0: 1: 1: 1].
**Rows 3 and 4**: As rows 1 and 2.
**Row 5:** P0 [0: 1: 1: 1], (P1, K12, P1) twice, P0 [0: 1: 1: 1].
**Row 6:** K0 [0: 1: 1: 1], (K1, P12, K1) twice, K0 [0: 1: 1: 1].
**Row 7:** P0 [0: 1: 1: 1], (P1, C6B, C6F, P1) twice, P0 [0: 1: 1: 1].
**Row 8:** As row 6.
**Rows 9 and 10**: As rows 1 and 2.

**Row 11**: As row 1.

**Row 12 (WS):** P2 [2: 3: 3: 3], P2tog, *P9, P2tog, rep from * to last 2 [2: 3: 3: 3] sts, P to end. 25 [25: 27: 27: 27] sts.
Change to 12mm (US 17) needles.
Join in yarn B.

**Row 13:** Using yarn B, knit.
Cont in patt as folls:

**Row 1 (WS):** Using yarn B P0 [0: 1: 1: 1], *using yarn A P1, using yarn B P3, rep from * to last 1 [1: 2: 2: 2] sts, using yarn A P1, using yarn B P0 [0: 1: 1: 1].

**Row 2:** Using yarn B K2 [2: 3: 3: 3], *using yarn A K1, using yarn B K3, rep from * to last 3 [3: 0: 0: 0] sts, (using yarn A K1, using yarn B K2) 1 [1: 0: 0: 0] times.
These 2 rows form patt for rest of sleeve.
Cont in patt, shaping sides by inc 1 st at each end of 4th and every foll 6th row to 33 [33: 35: 35: 31] sts, then on every foll – [-: -: -: 4th] row until there are - [-: -: -: 37] sts.
Cont straight until sleeve meas 44 [44: 45: 45: 45] cm, ending with RS facing for next row.

**Shape top**
Keeping patt correct, cast off 3 sts at beg of next 2 rows. 27 [27: 29: 29: 31] sts.

Dec 1 st at each end of next 3 rows, then on foll 4th row, then on every foll alt row until 17 sts rem, then on foll 3 rows, ending with RS facing for next row.
Cast off rem 11 sts.

MAKING UP
Press as described on the information page.
Join right shoulder seam using back stitch, or mattress stitch if preferred.

**Neckband**
With RS facing, using 10mm (US 15) needles and yarn A, pick up and knit 4 sts down left side of front neck, 12 [14: 14: 16: 16] sts from front, 4 sts up right side of front neck, 4 sts down right side of back neck, 13 [15: 15: 17: 17] sts from back, then 4 sts up left side of back neck. 41 [45: 45: 49: 49] sts.
**Row 1 (WS):** P1, *K1, P1, rep from * to end.
**Row 2:** K1, *P1, K1, rep from * to end.
**Row 3:** As row 1.
Cast off in rib.
See information page for finishing instructions, setting in sleeves using the set-in method.
Embroider french knots onto back and front following chart.

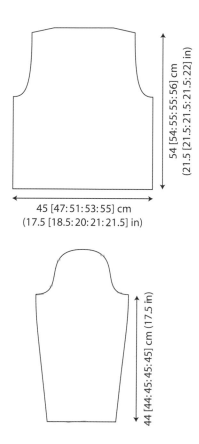

54 [54: 55: 55: 56] cm
(21.5 [21.5: 21.5: 21.5: 22] in)

45 [47: 51: 53: 55] cm
(17.5 [18.5: 20: 21: 21.5] in)

44 [44: 45: 45: 45] cm (17.5 in)

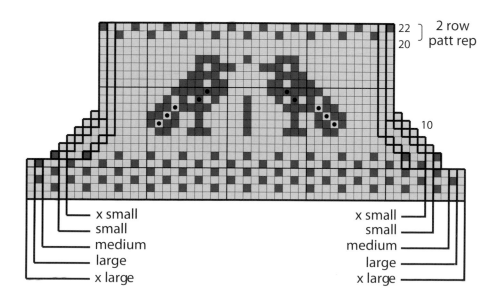

22 ⎤ 2 row
20 ⎦ patt rep

10

x small
small
medium
large
x large

x small
small
medium
large
x large

Key
■ A
□ B
⊡ french knot in A
⊡ french knot in B

No. 4

# AFGHAN
## MARTIN STOREY

**YARN**

**Rowan Big Wool and Biggy Print**

A  Big Flirty 037      4 x 100gm
B  Print Mermaid 260      1 x 100gm

**NEEDLES**

1 pair 12mm (US 17) needles

**FINISHED SIZE**

Completed scarf measures 26 cm (10 in) wide and 216 cm (85 in) long.

**TENSION**

8 sts and 12 rows to 10 cm measured over stocking stitch using 12mm (US 17) needles and yarn A.

SCARF

Using 12mm (US 17) needles and yarn A cast on 21 sts.
Work in g st for 2 rows, ending with RS facing for next row.

Cont in patt as folls:
**Row 1 (RS):** K2, K2tog, yfwd, K12, K2tog, yfwd, K3.
**Row 2 and every foll alt row**: K2, P17, K2.
**Row 3**: K4, yfwd, sl 1, K1, psso, K9, K2tog, yfwd, K4.
**Row 5**: K3, (yfwd, sl 1, K1, psso) twice, K7, (K2tog, yfwd) twice, K3.
**Row 7**: K4, (yfwd, sl 1, K1, psso) twice, K5, (K2tog, yfwd) twice, K4.
**Row 9**: K5, (yfwd, sl 1, K1, psso) twice, K3, (K2tog, yfwd) twice, K5.
**Row 11**: K6, (yfwd, sl 1, K1, psso) twice, K1, (K2tog, yfwd) twice, K6.
**Row 13**: K7, yfwd, sl 1, K1, psso, yfwd, K3tog, yfwd, K2tog, yfwd, K7.
**Row 15**: K8, yfwd, K3tog, yfwd, K2tog, yfwd, K8.
**Row 17:** K8, (K2tog, yfwd) twice, K9.
**Row 19:** K7, (K2tog, yfwd) twice, K1, yfwd, sl 1, K1, psso, K7.
**Row 21:** K6, (K2tog, yfwd) twice, K1, (yfwd, sl 1, K1, psso) twice, K6.
**Row 23:** K5, (K2tog, yfwd) twice, K3, (yfwd, sl 1, K1, psso) twice, K5.
**Row 25:** K4, (K2tog, yfwd) twice, K5, (yfwd, sl 1, K1, psso) twice, K4.
**Row 27:** K3, (K2tog, yfwd) twice, K7, (yfwd, sl 1, K1, psso) twice, K3.
**Row 29:** K2, (K2tog, yfwd) twice, K9, (yfwd, sl 1, K1, psso) twice, K2.
**Row 31:** K3, K2tog, yfwd, K11, yfwd, sl 1, K1, psso, K3.
**Row 32:** As row 2.
These 32 rows form patt.
Rep last 32 rows 7 times more, ending with RS facing for next row.
**Next row (RS):** Knit.
Cast off knitwise (on **WS**).

MAKING UP

Press as described on the information page. Using photograph as a guide, thread yarn B in and out of eyelet holes of patt.

# BERBER SCARF
## MARTIN STOREY

**YARN**
**Rowan Big Wool, Ribbon Twist and Biggy Print**

| | | |
|---|---|---|
| A | Big Latte 018 | 3 x 100gm |
| B | Ribbon Rustic 121 | 3 x 50gm |
| C | Print Cookie 243 | 3 x 100gm |
| D | Print Sheep 258 | 2 x 100gm |

**NEEDLES**
1 pair 12mm (US 17) needles
1 pair 15mm (US 19) needles

**FINISHED SIZE**
Completed scarf measures 30 cm (12 in) wide and 238 cm (93½ in) long.

**TENSION**
**Big Wool and Ribbon Twist**: 8 sts and 12 rows to 10 cm measured over stocking stitch using 12mm (US 17) needles.
**Biggy Print**: 6 sts and 9½ rows to 10 cm measured over stocking stitch using 15mm (US 19) needles.

SQUARE A (make 7)
Using 12mm (US 17) needles and yarn A cast on 12 sts.
Work in g st for 22 rows, ending with RS facing for next row.
Cast off.

SQUARE B (make 7)
Work as given for square A **but using yarn B**.

SQUARE C (make 7)
Using 15mm (US 19) needles and yarn C cast on 9 sts.
Work in g st for 18 rows, ending with RS facing for next row.
Cast off.

SQUARE D (make 7)
Work as given for square C **but using yarn D**.

MAKING UP
Press as described on the information page. Using photograph as a guide, join one square A to side of one square C, then join one square D to side of one square B. Sew cast-on edges of squares D and B to cast-off edges of squares A and C. Join rem squares to form a further 6 larger joined squares in this way, then join these larger squares to form one long strip. Using yarn A, oversew along all seams between squares. Using yarn A, work blanket stitch around entire outer edge of scarf.

No. 6

# RUSTIC
## CAROL MELDRUM

## YARN

|  | XS-S | M | L-XL |
|---|---|---|---|
| To fit bust | 81-86 | 91 | 97-102 cm |
|  | 32-34 | 36 | 38-40 in |

**Rowan Biggy Print**

| A | Slippery 235 | 12 | 13 | 14 | x 100gm |
|---|---|---|---|---|---|
| B | Mermaid 260 | 3 | 3 | 3 | x 100gm |

## NEEDLES
1 pair 12mm (US 17) needles
1 pair 20mm (US 36) needles
9.00mm (no 00) crochet hook

## BUTTONS – 3 toggles x 00345

## TENSION
5½ sts and 7 rows to 10 cm measured over stocking stitch using 20mm (US 36) needles.

## BACK
Using 20mm (US 36) needles and yarn A cast on 41 [43: 45] sts.
Beg with a K row, work in st st for 14 rows, ending with RS facing for next row.
Dec 1 st at each end of next and every foll 6th row to 35 [37: 39] sts, then on foll 4th row, then on foll 4 [5: 6] alt rows, then on foll row, ending with RS facing for next row. 23 sts.
**Shape shoulders and back neck**
**Next row (RS):** Cast off 3 sts, K until there are 5 sts on right needle and turn, leaving rem sts on a holder.
Work each side of neck separately.
Dec 1 st at beg of next row.
Cast off rem 4 sts.

With RS facing, rejoin yarn to rem sts, cast off centre 7 sts, K to end.
Complete to match first side, reversing shapings.

## LEFT FRONT
Using 20mm (US 36) needles and yarn A cast on 21 [22: 23] sts.
Beg with a K row, work in st st for 8 rows, ending with RS facing for next row.
**Divide for hand opening**
**Next row (RS):** K11 [12: 13] and turn, leaving rem 10 sts on a holder.
Work 11 rows on these sts, dec 1 st at beg of 6th of these rows and ending with RS facing for next row.
10 [11: 12] sts.
Do NOT break yarn but leave sts on another holder.
Return to 10 sts left on first holder, rejoin yarn with RS facing and work 12 rows (for centre front section), ending with RS facing for next row.
Break yarn.
**Join sections**
**Next row (RS):** work across 10 [11: 12] sts on second holder as folls: K2tog, K to end, then K 10 sts of centre front section.
19 [20: 21] sts.
Dec 1 st at beg of 6th and foll 4th row, then on foll 3 [4: 5] alt rows, ending with **WS** facing for next row.
14 sts.
**Shape neck**
Cast off 3 sts at beg of next row. 11 sts.

Dec 1 st at each end of next 2 rows, ending with RS facing for next row.
7 sts.
**Shape shoulder**
Cast off 3 sts at beg of next row.
Work 1 row.
Cast off rem 4 sts.

## RIGHT FRONT
Using 20mm (US 36) needles and yarn A cast on 21 [22: 23] sts.
Beg with a K row, work in st st for 8 rows, ending with RS facing for next row.
**Divide for hand opening**
**Next row (RS):** K10 and turn, leaving rem 11 [12: 13] sts on a holder.
Work 11 rows on these sts, ending with RS facing for next row.
Do NOT break yarn but leave sts on another holder.
Return to 11 [12: 13] sts left on first holder (for side section), rejoin yarn with RS facing and work 12 rows, dec 1 st at end of 7th of these rows and ending with RS facing for next row.
10 [11: 12] sts.
Break yarn.
**Join sections**
**Next row (RS):** K 10 sts on second holder, then work across 10 [11: 12] sts of side section as folls: K to last 2 sts, K2tog.
19 [20: 21] sts.
Complete to match left front, reversing shapings, working an extra row before beg of neck and shoulder shaping.

## MAKING UP

Press as described on the information page.

**Hand opening borders (all 4 alike)**

With RS facing, using 12mm (US 17) needles and yarn A, pick up and knit 10 sts along one row-end edge of hand opening.

Work in g st for 2 rows, ending with **WS** facing for next row.

Cast off knitwise (on **WS**).

Lay front border over back border and sew ends of borders in place.

See information page for finishing instructions.

### Trim

Using 9.00mm (no 00) crochet hook and yarn B make a chain at least 4 m long and fasten off.

Machine wash this strip at 60° (to felt and shrink it) and leave to dry. Once dry, attach trim to entire outer edge of cape, forming trim into 3 button loops along right front opening edge – position first loop 10 cm below neck edge, lowest loop 20 cm up from cast-on edge and rem loop evenly spaced between. Sew on toggles to correspond with loops.

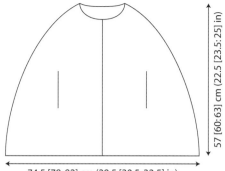

57 [60:63] cm (22.5 [23.5:25] in)

74.5 [78:82] cm (29.5 [30.5:32.5] in)

No. 7

# SWEETS
CAROL MELDRUM

### YARN
**Rowan Big Wool and Biggy Print**

A   Big Wool White Hot 001
        1   x 100gm

Oddments of Biggy Print in four contrast colours (Sherbert Dip 259, Razzle Dazzle 246, Pool Party 261 and Splash 248) for beads

### CROCHET HOOK
9.00mm (no 00) crochet hook

**EXTRAS** – necklace clasp or hook and eye (optional)

### FINISHED SIZE
Finished necklace can be made to any length. Once washed, shrunken and felted, distance between "beads" is approx 9 cm (3½ in).

### CROCHET ABBREVIATIONS
**ch** = chain; **yoh** = yarn over hook;
**sp** = space.

### NECKLACE
Using 9.00mm crochet hook and yarn A make 15 ch.

★★Join in contrast yarn and make "bead" as folls:
★yoh, treating last length of ch as a ch sp, insert hook into ch sp, yoh and draw loop through, yoh and draw through 2 loops, rep from ★ until 6 loops on hook, yoh and draw through all 6 loops. Break off contrast yarn and, using yarn A, make a further 15 ch.

Rep from ★★ until necklace is required length, noting that distance between each bead, once felted, will be approx 9 cm.

Once necklace is required length, fasten off.

### MAKING UP
Machine wash necklace at 60° (to felt and shrink it) and leave to dry. Join ends of strip (or attach necklace clasp or hook and eye).

No. 8

# ELLIE
## LUCINDA GUY

## YARN

|  | XS | S | M | L | XL |  |
|---|---|---|---|---|---|---|
| To fit bust | 81 | 86 | 91 | 97 | 102 | cm |
|  | 32 | 34 | 36 | 38 | 40 | in |

**Rowan Big Wool**

A  Black 008

|  | 5 | 5 | 5 | 6 | 6 | x 100gm |
|---|---|---|---|---|---|---|

B  Flirty 038

|  | 2 | 2 | 2 | 2 | 2 | x 100gm |
|---|---|---|---|---|---|---|

C  Ice Blue 021

|  | 1 | 1 | 2 | 2 | 2 | x 100gm |
|---|---|---|---|---|---|---|

D  Ginger Snap 039

|  | 1 | 1 | 1 | 1 | 1 | x 100gm |
|---|---|---|---|---|---|---|

## NEEDLES

1 pair 10mm (no 000) (US 15) needles
1 pair 12mm (US 17) needles
Cable needle

## TENSION

8 sts and 12 rows to 10 cm measured over stocking stitch, 9 sts and 10 rows to 10 cm measured over fairisle pattern using 12mm (US 17) needles.

## SPECIAL ABBREVIATIONS

**C4B** = slip next 2 sts onto cable needle and leave at back of work, K2, then K2 from cable needle; **C4F** = slip next 2 sts onto cable needle and leave at front of work, K2, then K2 from cable needle.

## BACK and FRONT (both alike)

Using 10mm (US 15) needles and yarn A cast on 39 [41: 43: 45: 47] sts.

Work in g st for 2 rows, ending with RS facing for next row.
Change to 12mm (US 17) needles.
Beg with a K row, work in st st for 22 [22: 24: 24: 26] rows, ending with RS facing for next row.
Beg and ending rows as indicated and using the **fairisle** techniques as described on the information page, cont in patt from chart, which is worked entirely in st st beg with a K row, as folls:
Work 12 [12: 10: 10: 8] rows, ending with RS facing for next row.

### Shape raglan armholes

Keeping chart correct, cast off 2 sts at beg of next 2 rows. 35 [37: 39: 41: 43] sts.
Dec 1 st at each end of next and foll 1 [3: 4: 4: 5] alt rows, then on every foll 4th row until 27 [27: 27: 29: 29] sts rem.
Inc 1 st at centre of next row, ending after chart row 26 and with RS facing for next row. 28 [28: 28: 30: 30] sts.
Break off contrasts and cont using yarn A **only**.
**Next row (RS):** K2 [2: 2: 3: 3], (C4B, C4F) 3 times, K2 [2: 2: 3: 3].
**Next row:** Purl.
**Next row:** K2tog, K0 [0: 0: 1: 1], (C4F, C4B) 3 times, K0 [0: 0: 1: 1], K2tog.
26 [26: 26: 28: 28] sts.
**Next row:** Purl.
Break yarn and leave sts on a holder.

## SLEEVES

Using 10mm (US 15) needles and yarn A cast

on 21 [21: 23: 23: 25] sts.
Work in g st for 2 rows, ending with RS facing for next row.
Change to 12mm (US 17) needles.
Beg with a K row, cont in st st, shaping sides by inc 1 st at each end of 5th and every foll 6th row to 33 [33: 31: 31: 31] sts, then on every foll – [–: 8th: 8th: 8th] row until there are – [–: 35: 35: 37] sts.
Work 1 row, ending with RS facing for next row.
Beg and ending rows as indicated, cont in patt from chart as folls:
Work 12 [12: 10: 10: 8] rows, ending with RS facing for next row.

### Shape raglan

Keeping chart correct, cast off 2 sts at beg of next 2 rows.
29 [29: 31: 31: 33] sts.
Dec 1 st at each end of next 5 rows, then on every foll alt row until 13 sts rem.
Inc 1 st at centre of next row, ending after chart row 26 and with RS facing for next row. 14 sts.
Break off contrasts and cont using yarn A **only**.
**Next row (RS):** K2tog, K1, C4B, C4F, K1, K2tog. 12 sts.
**Next row:** Purl.
**Next row:** K2tog, C4F, C4B, K2tog. 10 sts.
**Next row:** Purl.
Break yarn and leave sts on a holder.

## MAKING UP

Press as described on the information page.

Join both front and right back raglan seams using back stitch, or mattress stitch if preferred.

**Neckband**

With RS facing, using 10mm (US 15) needles and yarn A, K across 10 sts of left sleeve as folls: K1, (K2tog) 4 times, K1, K across 26 [26: 26: 28: 28] sts of front as folls: K1 [1: 1: 2: 2], K2tog, (K1, K2tog) 7 times, K2 [2: 2: 3: 3], K across 10 sts of right sleeve as folls: K1, (K2tog) 4 times, K1, then K across 26 [26: 26: 28: 28] sts of back as folls: K1 [1: 1: 2: 2], K2tog, (K1, K2tog) 7 times, K2 [2: 2: 3: 3]. 48 [48: 48: 52: 52] sts. Work in g st for 2 rows, ending with **WS**

facing for next row.
Cast off knitwise (on **WS**).
Join left back raglan and neckband seams.
See information page for finishing instructions, setting in sleeves using the set-in method.
Embroider french knots onto all pieces following chart.

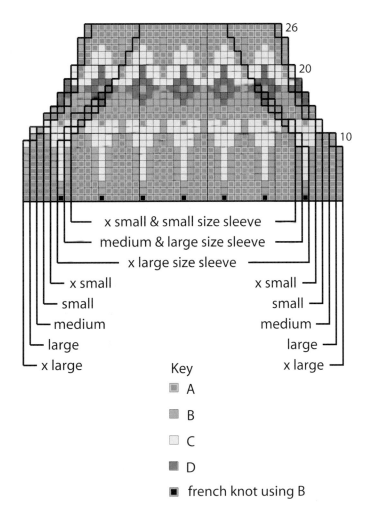

26
20
10

x small & small size sleeve
medium & large size sleeve
x large size sleeve

x small
small
medium
large
x large

x small
small
medium
large
x large

Key

■ A

■ B

□ C

■ D

■ french knot using B

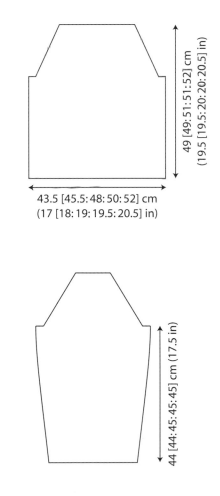

49 [49: 51: 51: 52] cm
(19.5 [19.5: 20: 20: 20.5] in)

43.5 [45.5: 48: 50: 52] cm
(17 [18: 19: 19.5: 20.5] in)

44 [44: 45: 45: 45] cm (17.5 in)

# LILLA

## LUCINDA GUY

## YARN

**Rowan Big Wool**

A  Whoosh 014          2 x 100gm
B  Bohemian 028        1 x 100gm

## NEEDLES

1 pair 10mm (no 000) (US 15) needles
Cable needle
6.00mm (no 4) (US J10) crochet hook

## BUTTONS – 2 x 00390

## FINISHED SIZE

Completed bag measures 30 cm (12 in) wide
and 24 cm (9½ in) deep.

## TENSION

12 sts and 12 rows to 10 cm measured over
pattern using 10mm (US 15) needles.

## SPECIAL ABBREVIATIONS

**C2B** = slip next st onto cable needle and leave
at back of work, K1, then K1 from cable needle;
**C2F** = slip next st onto cable needle and leave
at front of work, K1, then K1 from cable needle;
**Tw2R** = **on RS rows**, slip next st onto cable
needle and leave at back of work, K1, then P1
from cable needle, or **on WS rows**, slip next st
onto cable needle and leave at front of work, P1,
then K1 from cable needle; **Tw2L** = **on RS
rows**, slip next st onto cable needle and leave at
front of work, P1, then K1 from cable needle, or
**on WS rows**, slip next st onto cable needle and
leave at back of work, K1, then P1 from cable
needle; **MB** = (K1, yfwd, K1) all into next st,

turn and K3, turn and P3, turn and K3, turn and
sl 1, K2tog, psso.

## CROCHET ABBREVIATIONS

**ch** = chain; **dc** = double crochet;
**ss** = slip stitch.

BACK and FRONT (both alike)
Using 10mm (US 15) needles and yarn B cast
on 36 sts.
**Row 1 (WS):** Using yarn B, ★(K1, P1, K1) all
into next st, P3tog, rep from ★ to end.
**Row 2:** Using yarn B, purl.
Join in yarn A.
**Row 3:** Using yarn A, ★P3tog, (K1, P1, K1) all
into next st, rep from ★ to end.
**Row 4:** Using yarn A, purl.
**Rows 5 to 16:** As rows 1 to 4, 3 times.
Break off yarn B and cont using yarn A only.
**Row 17:** ★P2tog, P1, rep from ★ to end.  24 sts.
**Row 18:** Knit.
**Row 19:** (K5, P2, K5) twice.
**Row 20:** (P4, C2B, C2F, P4) twice.
**Row 21:** (K3, Tw2R, P2, Tw2L, K3) twice.
**Row 22:** (P2, Tw2R, C2B, C2F, Tw2L, P2) twice.
**Row 23:** (K1, Tw2R, K1, P4, K1, Tw2L, K1)
twice.
**Row 24:** (Tw2R, P1, Tw2R, K2, Tw2L, P1,
Tw2L) twice.
**Row 25:** (P1, K2, P1, K1, P2, K1, P1, K2, P1)
twice.
**Row 26:** (MB, P1, Tw2R, P1, K2, P1, Tw2L,
P1, MB) twice.
**Row 27:** (K2, P1, K2, P2, K2, P1, K2) twice.
**Row 28:** (P2, MB, P2, K2, P2, MB, P2) twice.

**Row 29:** Purl.
Cast off knitwise.

## MAKING UP

Press as described on the information page.
Join side and base seam using back stitch, or
mattress stitch if preferred, leaving cast-off
edges open.

**Edging**

With RS facing, using 6.00mm (US J10)
crochet hook and yarn B, rejoin yarn to upper
(cast-off) edge and work 1 round of dc around
upper edge of bag, working one dc into each
cast-off st and ending with ss to first dc. 48 sts.
**Next round (RS):** 1 ch (does NOT count as st),
★1 dc into each of next 2 dc, (1 dc, 1 ch and
1 dc) into next dc, rep from ★ to end, ss to first dc.
Fasten off.

**Handle**

Using 6.00mm (US J10) crochet hook and
yarn B, make 63 ch.
**Round 1 (RS):** 1 dc into 2nd ch from hook,
1 dc into each of next 60 ch, 3 dc into last ch,
working back along other side of foundation
ch, work 1 dc into each of next 60 ch, 2 dc
into next ch (this is same ch as used for dc at
beg of round), ss to first dc. 66 sts.
**Round 2:** 1 ch (does NOT count as st),
★1 dc into each of next 2 dc, (1 dc, 1 ch and
1 dc) into next dc, rep from ★ to end, ss to first dc.
Fasten off.
Using photograph as a guide, sew handle in
place to side seams of bag by attaching buttons
through both layers.
See information page for finishing instructions.

# TANGLE HAT

## MARTIN STOREY

**YARN**

**Rowan Chunky Print and Biggy Print**
A   Chunky Rhapsody 086   1 x 100gm
B   Biggy Tickle 237          1 x 100gm

**NEEDLES**

1 pair 8mm (no 0) (US 11) needles

**TENSION**

11 sts and 14 rows to 10 cm measured over stocking stitch using 8mm (US 11) needles and yarn A.

**SPECIAL ABBREVIATIONS**

**wyab** = with yarn at back of work;
**wyaf** = with yarn at front of work.

HAT

Using 8mm (US 11) needles and yarn A cast on 53 sts.

**Row 1 (RS):** Using yarn A, knit.
**Row 2:** Using yarn A, purl.
Join yarn B.
**Row 3:** Using yarn B, K1, (sl 1 purlwise wyab) 3 times, ★(sl 1 purlwise wyaf) 3 times, (sl 1 purlwise wyab) 3 times, rep from ★ to last st, K1.
**Row 4:** Using yarn B, P1, (sl 1 purlwise wyaf) 3 times, ★(sl 1 purlwise wyab) 3 times, (sl 1 purlwise wyaf) 3 times, rep from ★ to last st, P1.
**Rows 5 and 6:** As rows 1 and 2.
**Row 7:** Using yarn B, K1, (sl 1 purlwise wyaf) 3 times, ★(sl 1 purlwise wyab) 3 times, (sl 1 purlwise wyaf) 3 times, rep from ★ to last st, K1.
**Row 8:** Using yarn B, P1, (sl 1 purlwise wyab) 3 times, ★(sl 1 purlwise wyaf) 3 times, (sl 1 purlwise wyab) 3 times, rep from ★ to last st, P1.
Rep last 8 rows once more.

Break off yarn B and cont using yarn A **only**. Beg with a K row, work in st st until hat meas 15 cm, ending with RS facing for next row.
**Shape crown**
**Row 1 (RS):** (K10, K3tog) 4 times, K1. 45 sts.
**Row 2 and every foll alt row:** Purl.
**Row 3:** (K8, K3tog) 4 times, K1. 37 sts.
**Row 5:** (K6, K3tog) 4 times, K1. 29 sts.
**Row 7:** (K4, K3tog) 4 times, K1. 21 sts.
**Row 8:** P1, (P2tog) 10 times.
Break yarn and thread through rem 11 sts. Pull up tight and fasten off securely.

MAKING UP

Press as described on the information page. Join back seam.

# NOTHING
## ANTONI & ALISON

## YARN

|  | XS | S | M | L | XL |  |
|---|---|---|---|---|---|---|
| To fit bust | 81 | 86 | 91 | 97 | 102 | cm |
|  | 32 | 34 | 36 | 38 | 40 | in |

**Rowan Big Wool**

A  Smudge 019

|  | 6 | 6 | 7 | 7 | 8 | x 100gm |
|---|---|---|---|---|---|---|

B  Zing 037

|  | 1 | 1 | 1 | 1 | 1 | x 100gm |
|---|---|---|---|---|---|---|

C  Ginger Snap 039

|  | 1 | 1 | 1 | 1 | 1 | x 100gm |
|---|---|---|---|---|---|---|

D  Glamour 036

|  | 1 | 1 | 1 | 1 | 1 | x 100gm |
|---|---|---|---|---|---|---|

E  Flirty 037

|  | 1 | 1 | 1 | 1 | 1 | x 100gm |
|---|---|---|---|---|---|---|

## NEEDLES

1 pair 10mm (no 000) (US 15) needles
1 pair 12mm (US 17) needles

## TENSION

8 sts and 12 rows to 10 cm measured over stocking stitch using 12mm (US 17) needles.

## BACK

Using 10mm (US 15) needles and yarn A cast on 37 [39: 41: 43: 45] sts.
**Row 1 (RS):** K1, *P1, K1, rep from * to end.
**Row 2:** P1, *K1, P1, rep from * to end.
These 2 rows form rib.
Work in rib for a further 4 rows, ending with RS facing for next row.
Change to 12mm (US 17) needles.
Beg with a K row, work in st st for 4 rows, ending with RS facing for next row.

Beg and ending rows as indicated and using the **intarsia** method as described on the information page, cont in patt from chart for back, which is worked entirely in st st beg with a K row, as folls:
Work 28 rows, ending with RS facing for next row.
### Shape raglan armholes
Keeping chart correct, cast off 2 sts at beg of next 2 rows. 33 [35: 37: 39: 41] sts.
**Next row (RS):** K1, sl 1, K1, psso, patt to last 3 sts, K2tog, K1.
Working all raglan armhole decreases as set by last row, dec 1 st at each end of 2nd row. 31 [33: 35: 37: 39] sts.
Work 1 row, ending after chart row 34 and with RS facing for next row.
Beg with a K row, cont in st st using yarn A only as folls:
Dec 1 st at each end of next and foll 0 [2: 3: 3: 4] alt rows, then on every foll 4th row until 19 [19: 19: 21: 21] sts rem.
Work 1 row, ending with RS facing for next row.
Cast off.

## FRONT

Using 10mm (US 15) needles and yarn A cast on 37 [39: 41: 43: 45] sts.
Work in rib as given for back for 6 rows, ending with RS facing for next row.
Change to 12mm (US 17) needles.
Beg with a K row, work in st st until front matches back to beg of raglan armhole shaping, ending with RS facing for next row.

### Shape raglan armholes
Cast off 2 sts at beg of next 2 rows.
33 [35: 37: 39: 41] sts.
Working all raglan armhole decreases as set by back, dec 1 st at each end of next and foll 2 [4: 5: 5: 6] alt rows, then on every foll 4th row until 23 [23: 23: 25: 25] sts rem.
Work 1 row, ending with RS facing for next row.
### Shape neck
**Next row (RS):** K7 and turn, leaving rem sts on a holder.
Work each side of neck separately.
Dec 1 st at neck edge of next 2 rows, then on foll alt row **and at same time** dec 1 st at raglan armhole edge of 2nd row. 3 sts.
Work 1 row, ending with RS facing for next row.
**Next row (RS):** K1, sl 1, K1, psso. 2 sts.
**Next row:** P2.
**Next row:** K2tog and fasten off.
With RS facing, rejoin yarn to rem sts, cast off centre 9 [9: 9: 11: 11] sts, K to end. 7 sts.
Complete to match first side, reversing shapings.

## SLEEVES

Using 10mm (US 15) needles and yarn A cast on 17 [17: 19: 19: 21] sts.
Work in rib as given for back for 6 rows, ending with RS facing for next row.
Change to 12mm (US 17) needles.
Beg with a K row, work in st st, shaping sides by inc 1 st at each end of 3rd and every foll 6th row to 23 [23: 25: 25: 27] sts, then on

every foll 8th row until there are 29 [29: 31: 31: 33] sts.

Cont straight until sleeve meas 43 [43: 45: 45: 45] cm, ending with RS facing for next row.

**Shape raglan**

Cast off 2 sts at beg of next 2 rows.

25 [25: 27: 27: 29] sts.

Working all raglan armhole decreases as set by back, dec 1 st at each end of next and every foll 4th row to 19 [19: 21: 21: 23] sts, then on every foll alt row until 7 sts rem.

Work 1 row, ending with RS facing for next row.

Cast off rem 7 sts.

MAKING UP

Press as described on the information page.

Join both front and right back raglan seams using back stitch, or mattress stitch if preferred.

**Neckband**

With RS facing, using 10mm (US 15) needles and yarn A, pick up and knit 6 sts from left sleeve, 7 sts down left side of neck, 9 [9: 9: 11: 11] sts from front, and 7 sts up right side of neck, 6 sts from right sleeve, then 18 [18: 18: 20: 20] sts from back. 53 [53: 53: 57: 57] sts.

Beg with row 2, work in rib as given for back for 10 rows, ending with **WS** facing for next row.

Cast off in rib (on **WS**).

**Bow**

Using 10mm (US 15) needles and yarn A cast on 8 sts.

Beg with a K row, work in st st for 28 cm, ending with RS facing for next row.

Cast off.

**Bow centre**

Using 10mm (US 15) needles and yarn A cast on 4 sts.

Beg with a K row, work in st st for 10 rows, ending with RS facing for next row.

Cast off.

See information page for finishing instructions.

Join left back raglan and neckband seams.

Fold neckband in half to inside and loosely stitch in place. Join cast-on and cast-off edges of bow. Fold bow flat so that seam is at centre back. Wrap bow centre around bow, joining cast-on and cast-off edges at back. Sew bow to front of sweater as in photograph.

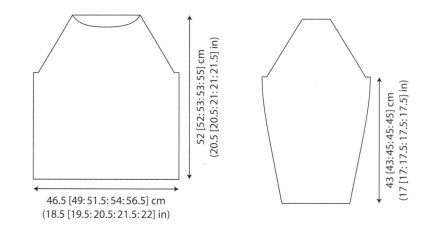

52 [52: 53: 53: 55] cm
(20.5 [20.5: 21: 21: 21.5] in)

46.5 [49: 51.5: 54: 56.5] cm
(18.5 [19.5: 20.5: 21.5: 22] in)

43 [43: 45: 45: 45] cm
(17 [17: 17.5: 17.5: 17.5] in)

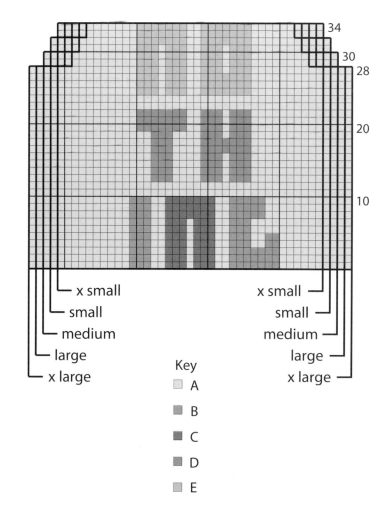

34
30
28
20
10

x small
small
medium
large
x large

x small
small
medium
large
x large

Key
- A
- B
- C
- D
- E

No. 12

# BERBER BAG
## MARTIN STOREY

**YARN**

**Rowan Big Wool and Biggy Print**

| | | |
|---|---|---|
| A | Big Tricky 030 | 1 x 100gm |
| B | Big Glamour 036 | 1 x 100gm |
| C | Print Pool Party 261 | 1x 100gm |
| D | Print Splash 248 | 1 x 100gm |
| E | Big Blue Velvet 026 | 1x 100gm |

**NEEDLES**

1 pair 10mm (no 000) (US 15) needles
1 pair 12mm (US 17) needles
1 pair 15mm (US 19) needles

**FINISHED SIZE**

Completed bag measures 30 cm
(12 in) square.

**TENSION**

**Big Wool**: 8 sts and 12 rows to 10 cm
measured over stocking stitch using 12mm
(US 17) needles.
**Biggy Print**: 6 sts and 9½ rows to 10 cm
measured over stocking stitch using 15mm

(US 19) needles.

SQUARE A (make 2)
Using 12mm (US 17) needles and yarn A cast
on 12 sts.
Work in g st for 22 rows, ending with RS
facing for next row.
Cast off.

SQUARE B (make 2)
Work as given for square A **but using
yarn B**.

SQUARE C (make 2)
Using 15mm (US 19) needles and yarn C cast
on 9 sts.
Work in g st for 18 rows, ending with RS
facing for next row.
Cast off.

SQUARE D (make 2)
Work as given for square C **but using
yarn D**.

HANDLES (make 2)
Using 10mm (US 15) needles and yarn E cast
on 30 sts.
Work in g st for 5 rows, ending with **WS**
facing for next row.
Cast off knitwise (on **WS**).

MAKING UP
Press as described on the information page.
Using photograph as a guide, join one square
B to side of one square D, then join one
square C to side of one square A. Sew cast-on
edges of squares C and A to cast-off edges of
squares B and D. Join rem squares to form a
further larger joined square in same way. Using
yarn E, oversew along all seams between
squares. Join larger squares along 3 sides,
leaving upper edge open. Using yarn E, work
blanket stitch around entire opening edge of
bag, and over side and base seams.
Sew row-end edges of handles inside upper
edges, positioning handles approx 3 cm in
from side seams.

# DAISY

## THERESA VENNING

**YARN**
**Rowan Big Wool Fusion and Big Wool**
A  Fusion Cyclamen 00003        1 x 100gm
B  Big White Hot 001             1 x 100gm

**NEEDLES**
1 pair 8mm (no 0) (US 11) needles
1 pair 10mm (no 000) (US 15) needles

**FASTENINGS** – 3 hooks and eyes

**FINISHED SIZE**
Completed belt is 7 cm (2¾ in) wide.

**TENSION**
Based on a stocking stitch tension of 8 sts and
12 rows to 10 cm using 12mm (US 17)
needles.

**BELT**
Using 8mm (US 11) needles and yarn A cast
on 7 sts.
**Row 1 (RS):** K1, (P1, K1) 3 times.
**Row 2:** As row 1.
These 2 rows form moss st.
Cont in moss st until belt fits neatly around
waist, ending with RS facing for next row.
Cast off in moss st.

FLOWERS (make 2)
Using 10mm (US 15) needles and yarn A cast
on 57 sts.
**Row 1 (WS):** Purl.
**Row 2:** K2, ★K1, slip this st back onto left
needle and lift next 8 sts on left needle over
this st and off left needle, (yfwd) twice, then K
same st again, K2, rep from ★ to end.
27 sts.
Break off yarn A and join in yarn B.
**Row 3:** P1, ★P2tog, P into front and back of
double yfwd of previous row, P1, rep from ★ to
last st, P1.

22 sts.
**Row 4:** (K2tog) 11 times.
**Row 5:** Purl.
Break yarn and thread through rem 11 sts. Pull
up tight and fasten off securely.

BOBBLES (make 6)
Using 8mm (US 11) needles and yarn A cast
on 1 st.
**Row 1 (RS):** (K1, yfwd, K1) all into st.
3 sts.
**Row 2:** P3.
**Row 3:** K3.
**Row 4:** P3tog and fasten off.

MAKING UP
Press as described on the information page.
Using photograph as a guide, sew flowers to
ends of belt, then sew 3 bobbles into centre of
each flower. Attach hooks and eyes to fasten
ends of belt.

# ERIN
## THERESA VENNING

## YARN

|  | XS | S | M | L | XL |  |
|---|---|---|---|---|---|---|
| To fit bust | 81 | 86 | 91 | 97 | 102 | cm |
|  | 32 | 34 | 36 | 38 | 40 | in |

**Rowan Big Wool Fusion**

7  7  7  8  8  x 100gm

(photographed in Gooseberry 00002)

## NEEDLES
1 pair 10mm (no 000) (US 15) needles
1 pair 12mm (US 17) needles
10mm (no 000) (US 15) circular needle
Cable needle

## TENSION
8 sts and 12 rows to 10 cm measured over
stocking stitch using 12mm (US 17) needles.

## SPECIAL ABBREVIATIONS
**C6B** = slip next 3 sts onto cable needle and
leave at back of work, K3, then K3 from cable
needle; **Cr5R** = slip next 2 sts onto cable
needle and leave at back of work, K3, then P2
from cable needle; **Cr5L** = slip next 3 sts onto
cable needle and leave at front of work, P2,
then K3 from cable needle; **MB** = (K1, yfwd,
K1, yfwd, K1) all into next st, turn and P5,
turn and K5, turn and P5, turn and sl 1, K1,
psso, K1, K2tog, turn and P3tog, turn
and K1.

## BACK and FRONT (both alike)
Using 10mm (US 15) needles cast on 84 [86:
88: 90: 92] sts.
**Row 1 (RS):** Knit.

**Row 2:** K15 [16: 17: 17: 18], (inc in next st)
3 times, K48 [48: 48: 50: 50], (inc in next st)
3 times, K to end. 90 [92: 94: 96: 98] sts.
Change to 12mm (US 17) needles.
## Place charts
**Row 1 (RS):** P6 [7: 8: 8: 9], work next 24 sts
as row 1 of chart, P12 [12: 12: 13: 13], P2tog,
K2 and place marker between these 2 sts,
P2tog tbl, P12 [12: 12: 13: 13], work next 24
sts as row 1 of chart, P to end.
88 [90: 92: 94: 96] sts.
**Row 2:** K6 [7: 8: 8: 9], work next 24 sts as
row 2 of chart, K13 [13: 13: 14: 14], P2
(marker is between these 2 sts), K13 [13: 13:
14: 14], work next 24 sts as row 2 of chart,
K to end.
These 2 rows set the sts − 2 charts on a rev
st st background with decreases either side of
centre 2 sts in st st.
Repeating the 12 row chart rep, cont as folls:
**Row 3:** Patt to within 3 sts of marker, P2tog,
K2 (marker is between these 2 sts), P2tog tbl,
patt to end.
86 [88: 90: 92: 94] sts.
**Row 4:** Patt to within 1 st of marker, P2
(marker is between these 2 sts), patt to end.
Dec 1 st at either side of marker as set on next
and foll 10 alt rows **and at same time** dec
1 st at each end of next and every foll 4th row,
ending after chart row 1 and with **WS** facing
for next row. 52 [54: 56: 58: 60] sts.
**Next row (WS):** P1 [2: 3: 3: 4], (P2tog, P2)
twice, (P2tog) 3 times, P2 [2: 2: 3: 3], P2tog,
(P2, P2tog) 4 times, P2 [2: 2: 3: 3], (P2tog)
3 times, (P2, P2tog) twice, P1 [2: 3: 3: 4].

Break yarn and leave rem 37 [39: 41: 43: 45] sts
on a holder, repositioning marker on centre st.

## SLEEVES
Using 10mm (US 15) needles cast on 27 [27:
29: 29: 31] sts.
**Row 1 (RS):** Knit.
**Row 2:** K12 [12: 13: 13: 14], (inc in next st)
3 times, K to end.
30 [30: 32: 32: 34] sts.
Change to 12mm (US 17) needles.
## Place chart
**Row 1 (RS):** P3 [3: 4: 4: 5], work next 24 sts
as row 1 of chart, P to end.
**Row 2:** K3 [3: 4: 4: 5], work next 24 sts as
row 2 of chart, K to end.
These 2 rows set the sts − chart on a rev st st
background.
Repeating the 12 row chart rep throughout,
work a further 35 rows, ending with **WS**
facing for next row.
**Next row (WS):** K3 [3: 4: 4: 5], P2, K7,
(P2tog) 3 times, K7, P2, K to end.
27 [27: 29: 29: 31] sts.
**Next row:** P3 [3: 4: 4: 5], K2, P7, K3, P7,
K2, P to end.
**Next row:** K3 [3: 4: 4: 5], P2, K7, P3, K7,
P2, K to end.
Last 2 rows set the sts for rest of sleeve.
Cont as set until sleeve meas 45 [45: 46:
46: 46] cm, ending with RS facing for
next row.
## Shape raglan
Cast off 4 sts at beg of next 2 rows.
19 [19: 21: 21: 23] sts.

Dec 1 st at each end of next and foll 1 [1: 2: 2: 3] alt rows, then on every foll 4th row until 9 sts rem.

Work 2 rows, ending with **WS** facing for next row.

**Next row (WS):** K3, P1, P2tog, K3.

Break yarn and leave rem 8 sts on a holder.

MAKING UP

Press as described on the information page. Join both side seams using back stitch, or mattress stitch if preferred.

**Neckband**

With RS facing, using 10mm (US 15) circular needle and beg 4 sts before left side seam, join sleeves to back and front whilst working first row of neckband as folls: holding RS of sleeve against WS of body (so that sleeves fall inside body) K tog 4th st before left side seam with first st of one sleeve, K tog next 7 sts of body (these are rem 3 sts of back and first 4 sts of front) with rem 7 sts of sleeve, K to within 2 sts of marked st, K2tog, K marked st, K2tog tbl, K to within 4 sts

of right side seam, K tog next 8 sts of body (these are rem 4 sts of front and first 4 sts of back) with 8 sts of other sleeve, K to within 2 sts of marked st, K2tog, K marked st, K2tog tbl, K to end.

70 [74: 78: 82: 86] sts.

**Next round (RS):** Purl.

**Next round:** (K to within 2 sts of marked st, K2tog, K marked st, K2tog tbl) twice, K to end. 66 [70: 74: 78: 82] sts.

Cast off purlwise (on RS).

See information page for finishing instructions.

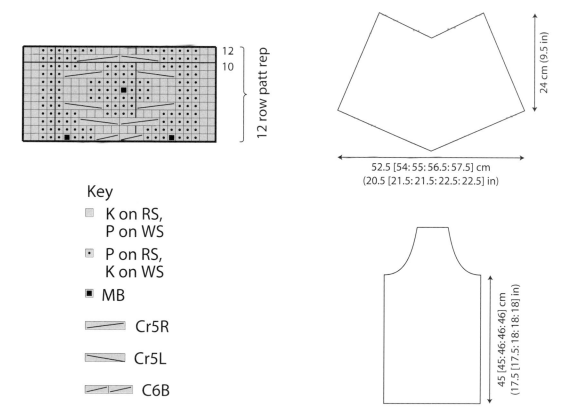

12 row patt rep

24 cm (9.5 in)

52.5 [54: 55: 56.5: 57.5] cm
(20.5 [21.5: 21.5: 22.5: 22.5] in)

45 [45: 46: 46: 46] cm
(17.5 [17.5: 18: 18: 18] in)

Key

K on RS, P on WS

P on RS, K on WS

MB

Cr5R

Cr5L

C6B

No. 15

# ELSA
## JENNIE ATKINSON

**YARN**

|  | XS | S | M | L | XL |
|---|---|---|---|---|---|
| To fit bust | 81 | 86 | 91 | 97 | 102 cm |
|  | 32 | 34 | 36 | 38 | 40 in |

**Rowan Big Wool Fusion**

7   7   7   8   8   x 100gm

(photographed in Baltic 00004)

**NEEDLES**

1 pair 10mm (no 000) (US 15) needles
1 pair 12mm (US 17) needles
Cable needle

**BUTTONS** - 7 x 00354

**TENSION**

8 sts and 12 rows to 10 cm measured over stocking stitch using 12mm (US 17) needles.

**SPECIAL ABBREVIATION**

**C8F** = slip next 4 sts onto cable needle and leave at front of work, K4, then K4 from cable needle.

BODY (worked in one piece from right cuff to left cuff)
Using 10mm (US 15) needles and cast on 20 [20: 20: 22: 22] sts.
**Row 1 (RS):** P1 [1: 1: 2: 2], *K2, P2, rep from * to last 3 [3: 3: 4: 4] sts, K2, P1 [1: 1: 2: 2].
**Row 2:** K1 [1: 1: 2: 2], *P2, K2, rep from * to last 3 [3: 3: 4: 4] sts, P2, K1 [1: 1: 2: 2].
These 2 rows form rib.
Work in rib for a further 18 rows, ending with

RS facing for next row.
Change to 12mm (US 17) needles.
Cont in patt as folls:
**Row 1 (RS):** Inc in first st, P5 [5: 5: 6: 6], K8, P5 [5: 5: 6: 6], inc in last st.
22 [22: 22: 24: 24] sts.
**Row 2:** K7 [7: 7: 8: 8], P8, K7 [7: 7: 8: 8].
**Row 3:** P7 [7: 7: 8: 8], K8, P7 [7: 7: 8: 8].
**Row 4:** As row 2.
**Row 5:** Inc in first st, P6 [6: 6: 7: 7], C8F, P6 [6: 6: 7: 7], inc in last st.
24 [24: 24: 26: 26] sts.
**Row 6:** K8 [8: 8: 9: 9], P8, K8 [8: 8: 9: 9].
**Row 7:** P8 [8: 8: 9: 9], K8, P8 [8: 8: 9: 9].
**Row 8:** As row 6.
These 8 rows form patt and beg sleeve shaping.
Cont in patt, inc 1 st at each end of next and every foll 4th row to 38 [38: 38: 40: 40] sts, then on foll 4 alt rows, then on foll 4 rows, taking inc sts into rev st st and ending with **WS** facing for next row. 54 [54: 54: 56: 56] sts.
Cast on 1 [2: 3: 3: 4] sts at beg of next 2 rows.
56 [58: 60: 62: 64] sts.
Place markers at both ends of last row to denote base of right sleeve seam.
Work a further 13 [15: 17: 19: 21] rows, ending with RS facing for next row.
**Divide for right front**
**Next row (RS):** Patt 26 [27: 28: 29: 30] sts and turn, leaving rem sts on a holder.
Work on this set of sts only for right front.
Dec 1 st at neck edge of next 2 rows, then on foll alt row, then on foll 3rd row.
22 [23: 24: 25: 26] sts.

Work a further 6 rows, ending with RS facing for next row.
Cast off.
**Shape back**
With RS facing, rejoin yarn to rem sts, cast off centre 4 sts (shoulder point is at centre of these 4 sts), patt to end.
26 [27: 28: 29: 30] sts.
Work 18 rows, dec 1 st at neck edge of 3rd of these rows.
25 [26: 27: 28: 29] sts.
Inc 1 st at neck edge of next row.
26 [27: 28: 29: 30] sts.
Work a further 2 rows, ending with RS facing for next row.
Break yarn and leave sts on a holder.
**Shape left front**
Using 12mm (US 17) needles and cast on 23 [24: 25: 26: 27] sts.
**Row 1 (RS):** Purl.
**Row 2:** Inc in first st, K to end.
**Row 3:** P to last st, inc in last st.
**Row 4:** Inc **purlwise** in first st, K to end.
26 [27: 28: 29: 30] sts.
**Join sections**
**Next row (RS):** P to last 2 sts of left front, K2, turn and cast on 4 sts (shoulder point is at centre of these 4 sts), turn and work across sts of back as folls: K2, P to end.
56 [58: 60: 62: 64] sts.
**Next row:** K24 [25: 26: 27: 28], P8, K to end.
Last row sets position of patt as for right front and sleeve.
Working first cable of this section on 3rd [5th: 7th: next: 3rd] row, work a further 12 [14: 16:

44

18: 20] rows, ending with RS facing for
next row.
Place markers at both ends of last row to
denote base of left sleeve seam.
Cast off 1 [2: 3: 3: 4] sts at beg of next 2 rows.
54 [54: 54: 56: 56] sts.
Dec 1 st at each end of next 5 rows, then on
foll 4 alt rows, then on every foll 4th row until
22 [22: 22: 24: 24] sts rem.
Work a further 3 rows, ending with RS facing
for next row.
Change to 10mm (US 15) needles.
**Next row (RS):** P2tog, P0 [0: 0: 1: 1], ★K2,
P2, rep from ★ to last 4 [4: 4: 5: 5] sts, K2,
P0 [0: 0: 1: 1], P2tog.
20 [20: 20: 22: 22] sts.
Beg with row 2, work in rib as given for right
cuff for 19 rows, ending with RS facing for
next row.
Cast off in rib.

MAKING UP
Press as described on the information page.
Join both sleeve seams using back stitch, or
mattress stitch if preferred, from markers to
cast-on or cast-off edges.
**Hem border**
With RS facing and using 10mm (US 15)
needles, beg and ending at front opening
edges, pick up and knit 13 [14: 15: 16: 17] sts
from lower edge of left front to sleeve seam,
34 [36: 38: 40: 42] sts from lower edge of back
to right sleeve seam, then 19 [20: 21: 22: 23] sts
from lower edge of right front.
66 [70: 74: 78: 82] sts.
**Row 1 (WS):** P2, ★K2, P2, rep from ★ to end.
**Row 2:** K2, ★P2, K2, rep from ★ to end.
These 2 rows form rib.
Work in rib for a further 5 rows, ending with
RS facing for next row.

Cast off in rib.
**Button band**
Using 10mm (US 15) needles cast on 5 sts.
Work in g st until band, when slightly
stretched, fits up entire left front opening edge,
from cast-off edge of hem border to neck
shaping, ending with RS facing for
next row.
Break yarn and leave sts on a holder.
Slip stitch band in place.
Mark positions for 4 buttons on this band –
first to come 2 cm up from lower edge, last to
come 2 cm below neck shaping, and rem 2
buttons evenly spaced between.
**Buttonhole band**
Using 10mm (US 15) needles cast on 5 sts.
Work in g st until band, when slightly
stretched, fits up entire right front opening
edge, from cast-off edge of hem border to
neck shaping, ending with RS facing for next
row and with the addition of 4 buttonholes to
correspond with positions marked for buttons
worked as folls:
**Buttonhole row (RS):** K2, yfwd, K2tog tbl,
K1.

When band is complete, do NOT break yarn.
**Collar**
With RS facing and using 10mm (US 15)
needles, K 5 sts of buttonhole band, pick up
and knit 15 sts up right side of front neck to
shoulder point, 20 sts from back to left
shoulder point, and 7 sts down left side of
front neck, then K 5 sts of button band. 52 sts.
**Row 1 (WS of body, RS of collar):** K5,
★P2, K2, rep from ★ to last 3 sts, K3.
**Row 2:** K7, ★P2, K2, rep from ★ to last 5 sts, K5.
These 2 rows set the sts – front opening edge
5 sts in g st with all other sts in rib.
Keeping sts correct as set, cont until collar
meas 4 cm from pick-up row, ending with RS
of body (WS of collar) facing for next row.
**Next row (buttonhole row):** K2, yfwd,
K2tog tbl, patt to end.
Cont straight until collar meas 12 cm.
Change to 12mm (US 17) needles.
Cont straight until collar meas 26 cm, making
a further 2 buttonholes as before when collar
meas 14 cm and 24 cm.
Cast off in patt.
See information page for finishing instructions.

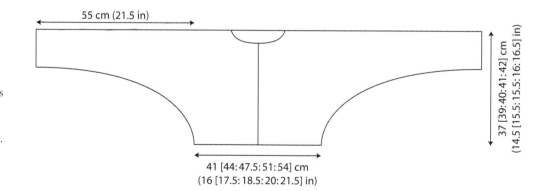

55 cm (21.5 in)

37 [39: 40: 41: 42] cm
(14.5 [15.5: 15.5: 16: 16.5] in)

41 [44: 47.5: 51: 54] cm
(16 [17.5: 18.5: 20: 21.5] in)

No. 16

# LAURA
## SARAH HATTON

## YARN

|  | XS | S | M | L | XL |  |
|---|---|---|---|---|---|---|
| To fit bust | 81 | 86 | 91 | 97 | 102 | cm |
|  | 32 | 34 | 36 | 38 | 40 | in |

**Rowan Big Wool Fusion**

|  | 6 | 7 | 8 | 8 | 9 | x 100gm |

(photographed in Source 00001)

## NEEDLES
1 pair 12mm (US 17) needles

## BUTTONS
7 x 00352

## TENSION
8 sts and 12 rows to 10 cm measured over stocking stitch using 12mm (US 17) needles.

**Pattern note**: As row end edges form actual finished front opening edges of garment, it is important these edges are kept neat. Therefore avoid joining in new balls of yarn at these edges.

## BACK
Using 12mm (US 17) needles cast on 39 [41: 43: 45: 47] sts.
**Row 1 (RS):** K3 [0: 1: 2: 3], *P1, K3, rep from * to last 0 [1: 2: 3: 0] sts, P0 [1: 1: 1: 0], K0 [0: 1: 2: 0].
**Row 2:** K1 [2: 3: 0: 1], *P1, K3, rep from * to last 2 [3: 0: 1: 2] sts, P1 [1: 0: 1: 1], K1 [2: 0: 0: 1].
These 2 rows form rib.
Work in rib for a further 6 rows, ending with RS facing for next row.

Beg with a K row, work in st st until back meas 34 [35: 35: 36: 36] cm, ending with RS facing for next row.
**Shape armholes**
Place markers at both ends of last row to denote base of armholes.
Dec 1 st at each end of next 4 rows.
31 [33: 35: 37: 39] sts.
Cont straight until armhole meas 21 [21: 22: 22: 23] cm, ending with RS facing for next row.
**Shape shoulders**
Cast off 5 [5: 5: 5: 6] sts at beg of next 2 rows, then 5 [5: 6: 6: 6] sts at beg of foll 2 rows.
Break yarn and leave rem 11 [13: 13: 15: 15] sts on a holder.

## LEFT FRONT
Using 12mm (US 17) needles cast on 23 [24: 25: 26: 27] sts.
**Row 1 (RS):** K3 [0: 1: 2: 3], *P1, K3, rep from * to end.
**Row 2:** K1, *P1, K3, rep from * to last 2 [3: 0: 1: 2] sts, P1 [1: 0: 1: 1], K1 [2: 0: 0: 1].
These 2 rows form rib.
Work in rib for a further 6 rows, ending with RS facing for next row.
**Row 9 (RS):** K to last 8 sts, rib 8.
**Row 10:** Rib 8, P to end.
These 2 rows set the sts.
Cont as set until left front matches back to beg of armhole shaping, ending with RS facing for next row.
**Shape armhole**
Place marker at end of last row to denote base of armhole.

Dec 1 st at armhole edge of next 4 rows.
19 [20: 21: 22: 23] sts.
Cont straight until 6 rows less have been worked than on back to beg of shoulder shaping, ending with RS facing for next row.
**Shape neck**
**Next row (RS):** Patt to last 6 [7: 7: 8: 8] sts and turn, leaving rem sts on a holder.
13 [13: 14: 14: 15] sts.
Dec 1 st at neck edge of next 3 rows.
10 [10: 11: 11: 12] sts.
Work 2 rows, ending with RS facing for next row.
**Shape shoulder**
Cast off 5 [5: 5: 5: 6] sts at beg of next row.
Work 1 row.
Cast off rem 5 [5: 6: 6: 6] sts.

## RIGHT FRONT
Using 12mm (US 17) needles cast on 23 [24: 25: 26: 27] sts.
**Row 1 (RS):** K3, *P1, K3, rep from * to last 0 [1: 2: 3: 0] sts, P0 [1: 1: 1: 0], K0 [0: 1: 2: 0].
**Row 2:** K1 [2: 3: 0: 1], *P1, K3, rep from * to last 2 sts, P1, K1.
These 2 rows form rib.
Work in rib for a further 6 rows, ending with RS facing for next row.
**Row 9 (RS):** Rib 8, K to end.
**Row 10:** P to last 8 sts, rib 8.
These 2 rows set the sts.
Complete to match left front, reversing shapings, working an extra row before beg of shoulder shaping and working first row of neck shaping as folls:

**Shape neck**

**Next row (RS):** Patt 6 [7: 7: 8: 8] sts and slip these sts onto a holder, patt to end.
13 [13: 14: 14: 15] sts.

SLEEVES

Using 12mm (US 17) needles cast on 17 [17: 19: 19: 21] sts.

**Row 1 (RS):** K2 [2: 3: 3: 0], *P1, K3, rep from * to last 3 [3: 0: 0: 1] sts, P1 [1: 0: 0: 1], K2 [2: 0: 0: 0].

**Row 2:** K0 [0: 1: 1: 2], *P1, K3, rep from * to last 1 [1: 2: 2: 3] sts, P1, K0 [0: 1: 1: 2].
These 2 rows form rib.
Work in rib for a further 6 rows, ending with RS facing for next row.
Beg with a K row, work in st st, shaping sides by inc 1 st at each end of next and every foll 6th row until there are 33 [33: 35: 35: 37] sts.
Cont straight until sleeve meas 46 [46: 47: 47: 47] cm, ending with RS facing for next row.

**Shape top**

Place markers at both ends of last row to denote top of sleeve seam.
Dec 1 st at each end of next 4 rows.
Cast off rem 25 [25: 27: 27: 29] sts.

MAKING UP

Press as described on the information page.
Join both shoulder seams using back stitch, or mattress stitch if preferred.

**Collar**

With RS facing and using 12mm (US 17) needles, slip 6 [7: 7: 8: 8] sts from right front holder onto right needle, rejoin yarn and pick up and knit 5 sts up right side of neck, work across 11 [13: 13: 15: 15] sts on back holder as folls: (K1, M1) 3 times, K1 [2: 2: 3: 3], (M1, K1) 3 times, M1, K1 [2: 2: 3: 3], (M1, K1) 3 times,

pick up and knit 5 sts down left side of neck, then patt 6 [7: 7: 8: 8] sts on left front holder.
43 [47: 47: 51: 51] sts.
Cont in rib as set by front opening edge sts until collar meas 19 cm.
Cast off in rib.
See information page for finishing instructions, setting in sleeves using the shallow set-in method.

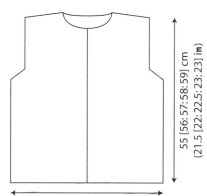

55 [56: 57: 58: 59] cm
(21.5 [22: 22.5: 23: 23] in)

49 [51.5: 54: 56.5: 59] cm
(19.5 [20.5: 21.5: 22: 23] in)

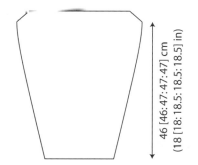

46 [46: 47: 47: 47] cm
(18 [18: 18.5: 18.5: 18.5] in)

# TANGLE TOP
## MARTIN STOREY

## YARN

| | XS | S | M | L | XL | |
|---|---|---|---|---|---|---|
| To fit bust | 81 | 86 | 91 | 97 | 102 | cm |
| | 32 | 34 | 36 | 38 | 40 | in |

**Rowan Chunky Print and Biggy Print**

| A Chunky Woolly 071 | | | | | | |
|---|---|---|---|---|---|---|
| | 4 | 4 | 5 | 5 | 5 | x 100gm |
| B Biggy Sh Dip 259 | | | | | | |
| | 1 | 1 | 1 | 1 | 1 | x 100gm |

## NEEDLES

1 pair 7mm (no 2) (US 10½) needles
1 pair 8mm (no 0) (US 11) needles

## TENSION

11 sts and 14 rows to 10 cm measured over stocking stitch using 8mm (US 11) needles and yarn A.

## SPECIAL ABBREVIATIONS

**wyab** = with yarn at back of work; **wyaf** = with yarn at front of work.

BACK
Using 7mm (US 10½) needles and yarn A cast on 45 [47: 51: 53: 57] sts.
Work in g st for 2 rows, ending with RS facing for next row.
Change to 8mm (US 11) needles.
**Row 1 (RS):** Using yarn A, knit.
**Row 2:** Using yarn A, purl.
Join in yarn B.
**Row 3:** Using yarn B, K1, (sl 1 purlwise wyaf) 0 [0: 2: 0: 0] times, (sl 1 purlwise wyab) 2 [3: 3: 0: 2] times, ★(sl 1 purlwise wyaf) 3 times, (sl 1

purlwise wyab) 3 times, rep from ★ to last 6 [1: 3: 4: 6] sts, (sl 1 purlwise wyaf) 3 [0: 2: 3: 3] times, (sl 1 purlwise wyab) 2 [0: 0: 0: 2] times, K1.
**Row 4:** Using yarn B, P1, (sl 1 purlwise wyab) 0 [0: 2: 0: 0] times, (sl 1 purlwise wyaf) 2 [3: 3: 0: 2] times, ★(sl 1 purlwise wyab) 3 times, (sl 1 purlwise wyaf) 3 times, rep from ★ to last 6 [1: 3: 4: 6] sts, (sl 1 purlwise wyab) 3 [0: 2: 3: 3] times, (sl 1 purlwise wyaf) 2 [0: 0: 0: 2] times, P1.
**Rows 5 and 6:** As rows 1 and 2.
**Row 7:** Using yarn B, K1, (sl 1 purlwise wyab) 0 [0: 2: 0: 0] times, (sl 1 purlwise wyaf) 2 [3: 3: 0: 2] times, ★(sl 1 purlwise wyab) 3 times, (sl 1 purlwise wyaf) 3 times, rep from ★ to last 6 [1: 3: 4: 6] sts, (sl 1 purlwise wyab) 3 [0: 2: 3: 3] times, (sl 1 purlwise wyaf) 2 [0: 0: 0: 2] times, K1.
**Row 8:** Using yarn B, P1, (sl 1 purlwise wyaf) 0 [0: 2: 0: 0] times, (sl 1 purlwise wyab) 2 [3: 3: 0: 2] times, ★(sl 1 purlwise wyaf) 3 times, (sl 1 purlwise wyab) 3 times, rep from ★ to last 6 [1: 3: 4: 6] sts, (sl 1 purlwise wyaf) 3 [0: 2: 3: 3] times, (sl 1 purlwise wyab) 2 [0: 0: 0: 2] times, P1.
These 8 rows form patt.
Work in patt for a further 8 rows, dec 1 st at each end of next row and ending with RS facing for next row.
43 [45: 49: 51: 55] sts.
Break off yarn B and cont using yarn A **only**.
Beg with a K row, work in st st, dec 1 st at each end of next and foll 6th row.
39 [41: 45: 47: 51] sts.

Work 7 rows, ending with RS facing for next row.
Inc 1 st at each end of next and every foll 6th row until there are 45 [47: 51: 53: 57] sts.
Cont straight until back meas 36 [37: 37: 38: 38] cm, ending with RS facing for next row.

**Shape armholes**
Cast off 3 [3: 4: 4: 5] sts at beg of next 2 rows.
39 [41: 43: 45: 47] sts.
Dec 1 st at each end of next 3 rows, then on foll 1 [1: 2: 2: 3] alt rows.
31 [33: 33: 35: 35] sts.
Cont straight until armhole meas 19 [19: 20: 20: 21] cm, ending with RS facing for next row.

**Shape shoulders and back neck**
Cast off 2 sts at beg of next 2 rows.
27 [29: 29: 31: 31] sts.
**Next row (RS):** Cast off 2 sts, K until there are 5 sts on right needle and turn, leaving rem sts on a holder.
Work each side of neck separately.
Cast off 3 sts at beg of next row.
Cast off rem 2 sts.
With RS facing, rejoin yarn to rem sts, cast off centre 13 [15: 15: 17: 17] sts, K to end.
Complete to match first side, reversing shapings.

FRONT
Work as given for back until 6 rows less have been worked than on back to beg of shoulder shaping, ending with RS facing for next row.

**Shape neck**

**Next row (RS):** K10 and turn, leaving rem sts on a holder.

Work each side of neck separately.

Dec 1 st at neck edge of next 3 rows, then on foll 1 alt row, ending with RS facing for next row. 6 sts.

**Shape shoulder**

Cast off 2 sts at beg of next and foll alt row. Work 1 row.

Cast off rem 2 sts.

With RS facing, rejoin yarn to rem sts, cast off centre 11 [13: 13: 15: 15] sts, K to end.

Complete to match first side, reversing shapings.

MAKING UP

Press as described on the information page.

Join right shoulder seam using back stitch, or mattress stitch if preferred.

**Neckband**

With RS facing, using 7mm (US 10½) needles and yarn A, pick up and knit 9 sts down left side of neck, 11 [13: 13: 15: 15] sts from front, 9 sts up right side of neck, then 19 [21: 21: 23: 23] sts from back.

48 [52: 52: 56: 56] sts.

Beg with K row, work in st st for 10 cm, ending with **WS** of collar (RS of body) facing for next row.

**Next row:** P4 [2: 2: 3: 3], M1P, ★P4, M1P, P4 [4: 4: 3: 3], M1P, rep from ★ to last 4 [2: 2: 4: 4] sts, P to end.

59 [65: 65: 71: 71] sts.

Change to 8mm (US 11) needles.

Cont in patt as folls:

**Row 1 (RS):** Using yarn A, knit.

**Row 2:** Using yarn A, purl.

Join in yarn B.

**Row 3:** Using yarn B, K1, (sl 1 purlwise wyab) 3 times, ★(sl 1 purlwise wyaf) 3 times, (sl 1 purlwise wyab) 3 times, rep from ★ to last st, K1.

**Row 4:** Using yarn B, P1, (sl 1 purlwise wyaf) 3 times, ★(sl 1 purlwise wyab) 3 times, (sl 1 purlwise wyaf) 3 times, rep from ★ to last st, P1.

**Rows 5 and 6:** As rows 1 and 2.

**Row 7:** Using yarn B, K1, (sl 1 purlwise wyaf) 3 times, ★(sl 1 purlwise wyab) 3 times, (sl 1 purlwise wyaf) 3 times, rep from ★ to last st, K1.

**Row 8:** Using yarn B, P1, (sl 1 purlwise wyab) 3 times, ★(sl 1 purlwise wyaf) 3 times, (sl 1 purlwise wyab) 3 times, rep from ★ to last st, P1.

These 8 rows form patt.

Work in patt for a further 9 rows, ending with **WS** of collar facing for next row.

Cast off knitwise (on **WS**).

Join left shoulder and collar seam, reversing collar seam for turn-back.

**Armhole borders (both alike)**

With RS facing, using 7mm (US 10½) needles and yarn A, pick up and knit 48 [48: 52: 52: 56] sts evenly all round armhole edge.

Work in g st for 2 rows, ending with **WS** facing for next row.

Cast off knitwise (on **WS**).

See information page for finishing instructions.

55 [56: 57: 58: 59] cm
(21.5 [22: 22.5: 23: 23] in)

41 [42.5: 46.5: 48: 52] cm
(16 [16.5: 18.5: 19: 20.5] in)

No. 18

# ULLA
## LUCINDA GUY

## YARN
**Rowan Big Wool**

A  Smoky 007      2 x 100gm
B  Zing 037        1 x 100gm
C  Pistachio 029   1 x 100gm
D  Whoosh 014      1 x 100gm

## NEEDLES
1 pair 10mm (no 000) (US 15) needles
1 pair 12mm (US 17) needles
Cable needle

**EXTRAS** – 1 button. Piece of lining fabric
35 cm x 50 cm. Matching sewing thread.

## FINISHED SIZE
Completed bag measures 28 cm (11 in) square.

## TENSION
9 sts and 10 rows to 10 cm measured over
patterned stocking stitch using 12mm (US 17)
needles.

## SPECIAL ABBREVIATIONS
**C4B** = slip next 2 sts onto cable needle and
leave at back of work, K2, then K2 from cable
needle; **C4F** = slip next 2 sts onto cable
needle and leave at front of work, K2, then K2
from cable needle.

## SIDES (make 2)
Using 12mm (US 17) needles and yarn A cast
on 25 sts.
Using the **fairisle** technique as described on the
information page, work in patt from chart, which
is worked entirely in st st beg with a K row, for

20 rows, ending with RS facing for next row.
Cast off.

## BORDER
Using 10mm (US 15) needles and yarn A cast
on 10 sts.
**Row 1 (RS):** Knit.
**Row 2 and every foll alt row**: K1, P8, K1.
**Row 3**: K1, C4B, C4F, K1.
**Row 5**: K1, C4F, C4B, K1.
**Row 6**: As row 2.
These 6 rows form patt.
Cont in patt until border meas 55 cm, ending
with RS facing for next row.
Cast off.

## HANDLE
Using 10mm (US 15) needles and yarn A cast
on 10 sts.
Work in patt as given for border for 40 cm,
ending with RS facing for next row.

Cast off.

## MAKING UP
Press as described on the information page.
From lining fabric, cut out pieces same size as
sides, adding seam allowance along all edges.
Embroider french knots onto sides as indicated
on chart. Join sides along row-end and cast-on
edges using back stitch, or mattress stitch if
preferred, leaving cast-off edges open. Join
ends of border, then sew border to cast-off
edges of sides. Sew ends of handle inside upper
edge.

Join lining pieces in same way as for knitted
side pieces. Fold seam allowance to WS around
upper edge. Slip lining inside bag and slip st
upper edge in place to border seam. Using
photograph as a guide, attach button to fasten
upper edge, pushing button through border to
form buttonhole.

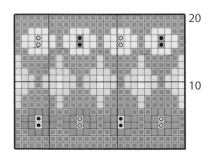

### Key
■ A
■ B
☐ C
☐ D
● French knot using B
◉ French knot using C
● French knot using D

No. 19

# PINKIE

CAROL MELDRUM

**YARN**
**Rowan Biggy Print**
A  Tickle 237     1 x 100gm
B  Giddy 239     1 x 100gm

**CROCHET HOOK**
9.00mm (no 00) crochet hook

**EXTRAS** – 1 safety pin or brooch back

**FINISHED SIZE**
Finished corsage, once washed, shrunken
and felted, measures approx 12 cm (4½ in) in
diameter.

**CROCHET ABBREVIATIONS**
**ch** = chain; **ss** = slip stitch.

CORSAGE
Using 9.00mm crochet hook and yarn A make
6 ch join with a ss to form a ring.
**Round 1:** (10 ch, 1 ss into ring) 6 times,
working last ss into same place as ss that closed
ring.
6 petals.
Fasten off.

Join in yarn B with a ss into base ring between
2 ss of previous round and, working between ss
of previous round behind first set of petals,
cont as folls:
**Round 2:** (15 ch, 1 ss into ring between next
2 ss), working last ss into same place as first ss.
6 petals.
Fasten off.

MAKING UP
Machine wash corsage at 60° (to felt and
shrink it) and leave to dry. Once dry, attach
safety pin, or brooch back, to back.

No. 20

# YULAH
## LEAH SUTTON

## YARN

|  | XS | S | M | L | XL |  |
|---|---|---|---|---|---|---|
| To fit bust | 81 | 86 | 91 | 97 | 102 | cm |
|  | 32 | 34 | 36 | 38 | 40 | in |

**Rowan Big Wool and Big Wool Tuft**

A  Big Smudge 019

|  | 5 | 5 | 6 | 6 | 6 | x 100gm |
|---|---|---|---|---|---|---|

B  Tuft P Puff 061

|  | 8 | 8 | 9 | 9 | 10 | x 50gm |
|---|---|---|---|---|---|---|

## NEEDLES
1 pair 10mm (no 000) (US 15) needles
1 pair 12mm (US 17) needles

## TENSION
8 sts and 12 rows to 10 cm measured over stocking stitch using 12mm (US 17) needles and yarn A.

## BACK
Using 12mm (US 17) needles and yarn A cast on 46 [48: 50: 52: 54] sts.
**Row 1 (RS):** Using yarn A, K1, K2tog, K4 [5: 6: 7: 8], yfwd, (K2, yfwd, K5, sl 1, K2tog, psso, K5, yfwd) twice, K2, yfwd, K4 [5: 6: 7: 8], K2tog tbl, K1.
**Row 2:** Using yarn A, purl.
Join in yarn B.
**Row 3:** Using yarn B, K1, K2tog, K4 [5: 6: 7: 8], yfwd, (K2, yfwd, K5, sl 1, K2tog, psso, K5, yfwd) twice, K2, yfwd, K4 [5: 6: 7: 8], K2tog tbl, K1.
**Row 4:** Using yarn B, purl.
**Rows 5 to 8**: As rows 1 to 4.
**Row 9:** Using yarn A, K1, sl 1, K2tog, psso,

K3 [4: 5: 6: 7], yfwd, (K2, yfwd, K5, sl 1, K2tog, psso, K5, yfwd) twice, K2, yfwd, K3 [4: 5: 6: 7], sl 1, K2tog, psso, K1.
44 [46: 48: 50: 52] sts.
**Row 10:** As row 2.
**Row 11:** Using yarn B, K1, K2tog, K3 [4: 5: 6: 7], yfwd, (K2, yfwd, K5, sl 1, K2tog, psso, K5, yfwd) twice, K2, yfwd, K3 [4: 5: 6: 7], K2tog tbl, K1.
**Row 12:** As row 4.
**Row 13:** Using yarn A, K1, sl 1, K2tog, psso, K2 [3: 4: 5: 6], yfwd, (K2, yfwd, K5, sl 1, K2tog, psso, K5, yfwd) twice, K2, yfwd, K2 [3: 4: 5: 6], sl 1, K2tog, psso, K1.
42 [44: 46: 48: 50] sts.
**Row 14:** As row 2.
**Row 15:** Using yarn B, K1, K2tog, K2 [3: 4: 5: 6], yfwd, (K2, yfwd, K5, sl 1, K2tog, psso, K5, yfwd) twice, K2, yfwd, K2 [3: 4: 5: 6], K2tog tbl, K1.
**Row 16:** As row 4.
Break off yarn B and cont using yarn A **only**.
**Row 17 (RS):** K4 [5: 6: 7: 8], (sl 1, K2tog, psso, K5) 4 times, sl 1, K2tog, psso, K to end.
32 [34: 36: 38: 40] sts.
Beg with a **P** row, work in st st, shaping side seams by inc 1 st at each end of 6th and foll 8th row.
36 [38: 40: 42: 44] sts.
Cont straight until back meas 20 cm **from last row worked using yarn B**, ending with RS facing for next row.
**Shape raglan armholes**
Cast off 3 sts at beg of next 2 rows.
30 [32: 34: 36: 38] sts.

Dec 1 st at each end of next and every foll alt row until 16 [18: 18: 20: 20] sts rem, then on foll 4th row.
14 [16: 16: 18: 18] sts.
Work 3 rows, ending with RS facing for next row.
Cast off.

## LEFT FRONT
Using 12mm (US 17) needles and yarn A cast on 25 [26: 27: 28: 29] sts.
**Row 1 (RS):** Using yarn A, K1, K2tog, K4 [5: 6: 7: 8], yfwd, K2, yfwd, K5, sl 1, K2tog, psso, K5, yfwd, K3.
**Row 2:** Using yarn A, K2, P to end.
Join in yarn B.
**Row 3:** Using yarn B, K1, K2tog, K4 [5: 6: 7: 8], yfwd, K2, yfwd, K5, sl 1, K2tog, psso, K5, yfwd, K3.
**Row 4:** Using yarn B, K2, P to end.
**Rows 5 to 8**: As rows 1 to 4.
**Row 9:** Using yarn A, K1, sl 1, K2tog, psso, K3 [4: 5: 6: 7], yfwd, K2, yfwd, K5, sl 1, K2tog, psso, K5, yfwd, K3.
24 [25: 26: 27: 28] sts.
**Row 10:** As row 2.
**Row 11:** Using yarn B, K1, K2tog, K3 [4: 5: 6: 7], yfwd, K2, yfwd, K5, sl 1, K2tog, psso, K5, yfwd, K3.
**Row 12:** As row 4.
**Row 13:** Using yarn A, K1, sl 1, K2tog, psso, K2 [3: 4: 5: 6], yfwd, K2, yfwd, K5, sl 1, K2tog, psso, K5, yfwd, K3.
23 [24: 25: 26: 27] sts.
**Row 14:** As row 2.

**Row 15:** Using yarn B, K1, K2tog, K2 [3: 4: 5: 6], yfwd, K2, yfwd, K5, sl 1, K2tog, psso, K5, yfwd, K3.
**Row 16:** As row 4.
Break off yarn B and cont using yarn A **only**.
**Row 17 (RS):** K1, K2tog, K4 [5: 6: 7: 8], (sl 1, K2tog, psso, K5) twice.
18 [19: 20: 21: 22] sts.
**Row 18:** K2, P to end.
**Row 19:** Knit.
Last 2 rows set the sts – front opening edge 2 sts in g st with all other sts in st st.
Cont as set, shaping side seam by inc 1 st at beg of 4th row.
19 [20: 21: 22: 23] sts.
Work 1 row, ending with RS facing for next row.
Join in yarn B and, using the **intarsia** technique as described on the information page, cont as folls:
**Row 25 (RS):** Using yarn A K11 [11: 12: 12: 13], using yarn B K1, using yarn A K to end.
**Row 26:** Using yarn A, K2, P to end.
These 2 rows form patt for rem of left front.
Cont in patt, inc 1 st at beg of 5th row.
20 [21: 22: 23: 24] sts.
Cont straight until left front matches back to beg of raglan armhole shaping, ending with RS facing for next row.

**Shape raglan armhole**
Keeping patt correct, cast off 3 sts at beg of next row.
17 [18: 19: 20: 21] sts.
Work 1 row.
Dec 1 st at beg of next and foll 2 alt rows.
14 [15: 16: 17: 18] sts.
Work 1 row, ending with RS facing for next row.

**Shape front slope**
Dec 1 st at end of next row and at same edge on foll 2 rows, then on foll 3 [5: 5: 6: 6] alt rows, then on foll 4th [–: –: –: –] row **and at same time** dec 1 st at raglan armhole edge of next and foll 3 [3: 4: 4: 5] alt rows, then on foll 4th row.
2 sts.
Work 1 [1: 3: 1: 3] rows, ending with RS facing for next row.
**Next row (RS):** K2tog and fasten off.

RIGHT FRONT
Using 12mm (US 17) needles and yarn A cast on 25 [26: 27: 28: 29] sts.
**Row 1 (RS):** Using yarn A, K3, yfwd, K5, sl 1, K2tog, psso, K5, yfwd, K2, yfwd, K4 [5: 6: 7: 8], K2tog tbl, K1.
**Row 2:** Using yarn A, P to last 2 sts, K2.
Join in yarn B.
**Row 3:** Using yarn B, K3, yfwd, K5, sl 1, K2tog, psso, K5, yfwd, K2, yfwd, K4 [5: 6: 7: 8], K2tog tbl, K1.
**Row 4:** Using yarn B, P to last 2 sts, K2.
**Rows 5 to 8:** As rows 1 to 4.
**Row 9:** Using yarn A, K3, yfwd, K5, sl 1, K2tog, psso, K5, yfwd, K2, yfwd, K3 [4: 5: 6: 7], sl 1, K2tog, psso, K1.
24 [25: 26: 27: 28] sts.
**Row 10:** As row 2.
**Row 11:** Using yarn B, K3, yfwd, K5, sl 1, K2tog, psso, K5, yfwd, K2, yfwd, K3 [4: 5: 6: 7], K2tog tbl, K1.
**Row 12:** As row 4.
**Row 13:** Using yarn A, K3, yfwd, K5, sl 1, K2tog, psso, K5, yfwd, K2, yfwd, K2 [3: 4: 5: 6], sl 1, K2tog, psso, K1. 23 [24: 25: 26: 27] sts.
**Row 14:** As row 2.
**Row 15:** Using yarn B, K3, yfwd, K5, sl 1, K2tog, psso, K5, yfwd, K2, yfwd, K2 [3: 4: 5: 6], K2tog tbl, K1.
**Row 16:** As row 4.
Break off yarn B and cont using yarn A **only**.
**Row 17 (RS):** (K5, sl 1, K2tog, psso) twice, K to last 3 sts, K2tog tbl, K1.
18 [19: 20: 21: 22] sts.
**Row 18:** P to last 2 sts, K2.
**Row 19:** Knit.
Last 2 rows set the sts – front opening edge 2 sts in g st with all other sts in st st.
Cont as set, shaping side seam by inc 1 st at end of 4th row.
19 [20: 21: 22: 23] sts.
Work 3 rows, ending with RS facing for next row.
Join in yarn B and, using the **intarsia** technique as described on the information page, cont as folls:
**Row 27 (RS):** Using yarn A K4 [5: 5: 6: 6], bring yarn B to front (RS) of work, using yarn A K7, take yarn B to back (WS) of work, using yarn A K to end.

**Row 28:** Using yarn A, P to last 2 sts, K2.
Inc 1 st at end of 3rd of these rows, rep rows 27 and 28, 3 times more and then row 27 again, ending with **WS** facing for next row.
20 [21: 22: 23: 24] sts.
**Row 36 (WS):** Using yarn A P12 [12: 13: 13: 14], using yarn B slip right needle point under 5 strands of yarn B running across RS (back) of work and P tog these 5 strands with next st, using yarn A P to last 2 sts, K2.
**Row 37:** Using yarn A K7 [8: 8: 9: 9], using yarn B K1, using yarn A K to end.
**Row 38:** Using yarn A, P to last 2 sts, K2.
Last 2 rows form patt for rem of right front.
Complete to match left front, reversing shapings, working an extra row before beg of raglan armhole shaping.

SLEEVES
Using 12mm (US 17) needles and yarn A cast on 39 [39: 41: 41: 43] sts.
**Row 1 (RS):** Using yarn A, K1, yfwd, K4 [4: 5: 5: 6], (sl 1, K2tog, psso, K4, yfwd, K2, yfwd, K4) twice, sl 1, K2tog, psso, K4 [4: 5: 5: 6], yfwd, K1.
**Row 2:** Using yarn A, purl.
Join in yarn B.
**Row 3:** Using yarn B, K1, yfwd, K4 [4: 5: 5: 6], (sl 1, K2tog, psso, K4, yfwd, K2, yfwd, K4) twice, sl 1, K2tog, psso, K4 [4: 5: 5: 6], yfwd, K1.
**Row 4:** Using yarn B, purl.
Rep last 4 rows 4 times more, then rows 1 and 2 again.
**Row 23:** Using yarn B, K5 [5: 6: 6: 7], (sl 1, K2tog, psso, K4, yfwd, K2, yfwd, K4) twice, sl 1, K2tog, psso, K5 [5: 6: 6: 7].
37 [37: 39: 39: 41] sts.
**Row 24:** Using yarn B, purl.
**Row 25:** Using yarn A, K1, yfwd, K3 [3: 4: 4: 5], (sl 1, K2tog, psso, K4, yfwd, K2, yfwd, K4) twice, sl 1, K2tog, psso, K3 [3: 4: 4: 5], yfwd, K1.
**Row 26:** Using yarn A, purl.
**Row 27:** Using yarn B, K1, yfwd, K3 [3: 4: 4: 5], (sl 1, K2tog, psso, K4, yfwd, K2, yfwd, K4) twice, sl 1, K2tog, psso, K3 [3: 4: 4: 5], yfwd, K1.
**Row 28:** Using yarn B, purl.
Rep rows 25 to 28, 3 times more.

**Row 41:** Using yarn A, K4 [4: 5: 5: 6], (sl 1, K2tog, psso, K4, yfwd, K2, yfwd, K4) twice, sl 1, K2tog, psso, K4 [4: 5: 5: 6].
35 [35: 37: 37: 39] sts.
**Row 42:** Using yarn A, purl.
**Row 43:** Using yarn B, K1, yfwd, K2 [2: 3: 3: 4], (sl 1, K2tog, psso, K4, yfwd, K2, yfwd, K4) twice, sl 1, K2tog, psso, K2 [2: 3: 3: 4], yfwd, K1.
**Row 44:** Using yarn B, purl.
**Row 45:** Using yarn A, K1, yfwd, K2 [2: 3: 3: 4], (sl 1, K2tog, psso, K4, yfwd, K2, yfwd, K4) twice, sl 1, K2tog, psso, K2 [2: 3: 3: 4], yfwd, K1.
**Row 46:** Using yarn A, purl.
Rows 43 to 46 form patt for rem of sleeve.
Cont in patt until sleeve meas 48 [48: 49: 49: 49] cm, ending with RS facing for next row.
**Shape raglan**
Keeping patt correct, cast off 3 sts at beg of next 2 rows.
29 [29: 31: 31: 33] sts.
Dec 1 st at each end of next and every foll alt row to 13 sts, then on foll 4th row.
11 sts.
Work 1 row, ending with RS facing for next row.
Cast off.

MAKING UP
Press as described on the information page. Join all raglan seams using back stitch, or mattress stitch if preferred.
**Neckband**
With RS facing, using 10mm (US 15) needles and yarn B, beg and ending at front opening edges, pick up and knit 14 [14: 15: 15: 16] sts up right front slope, 9 sts from right sleeve, 10 [11: 11: 12: 12] sts from back, 9 sts from left

sleeve, then 14 [14: 15: 15: 16] sts down left front slope.
56 [57: 59: 60: 62] sts.
**Row 1 (WS):** Knit.
**Row 2:** K1, K2tog, K to last 3 sts, K2tog tbl, K1.
Rep last 2 rows 3 times more.
Cast off rem 48 [49: 51: 52: 54] sts knitwise (on **WS**).
See information page for finishing instructions.

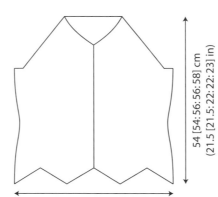

45 [47.5: 50: 52.5: 55] cm
(17.5 [18.5: 19.5: 20.5: 21.5] in)

54 [54: 56: 56: 58] cm
(21.5 [21.5: 22: 22: 23] in)

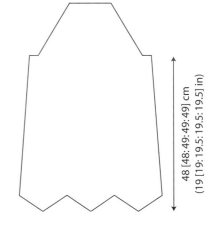

48 [48: 49: 49: 49] cm
(19 [19: 19.5: 19.5: 19.5] in)

AUSTRALIA:
Australian Country Spinners
314 Albert Street
Brunswick
Victoria 3056
Tel: (03) 9380 3888
Email: sales@auspinners.com.au

BELGIUM:
Pavan
Meerlaanstraat 73
B9860 Balegem (Oosterzele)
Tel: (32) 9 221 8594
Email: pavan@pandora.be

CANADA:
Diamond Yarn
9697 St Laurent, Montreal
Quebec, H3L 2N1
Tel: (514) 388 6188

Diamond Yarn (Toronto),
155 Martin Ross, Unit 3
Toronto
Ontario, M3J 2L9
Tel: (416) 736 6111
Email: diamond@diamondyarn.com
www.diamondyarns.com

DENMARK
Individual stockists please contact
Rowan for details

FRANCE:
Elle Tricot
8 Rue du Coq
67000 Strasbourg
Tel: (33) 3 88 23 03 13
Email: elletricot@agat.net
www.elletricote.com

GERMANY:
Wolle & Design
Wolfshovener Strasse 76
52428 Julich-Stetternich
Tel: (49) 2461 54735
Email: Info@wolleunddesign.de
www.wolleunddesign.de

Coats GMbH
Eduardstrasse 44
D-73084 Salach
Tel: (49) 7162 / 14-346
www.coatsgmbh.de

HOLLAND:
de Afstap
Oude Leliestraat 12
1015 AW Amsterdam
Tel: (31) 20 6231445

HONG KONG:
East Unity Co Ltd
Unit B2, 7/F Block B
Kailey Industrial Centre
12 Fung Yip Street, Chai Wan
Tel: (852) 2869 7110
Fax: (852) 2537 6952
Email: eastuni@netvigator.com

ICELAND:
Storkurinn
Laugavegi 59
101 Reykjavik
Tel: (354) 551 8258
Fax: (354) 562 8252
Email: malin@mmedia.is

ITALY:
D.L. srl
Via Piave, 24 – 26, 20016 Pero
Milan
Tel: (39) 02 339 10 180.

FINLAND:
Oy Nordia Produkter Ab
Mikkolantie 1
00640 Helsinki
Tel: (358) 9 777 4272
Email: info@nordiaprodukter.fi

JAPAN:
Puppy Co Ltd
T151-0051
3-16-5 Sendagaya
Shibuyaku, Tokyo
Tel: (81) 3 3490 2827
Email: info@rowan-jaeger.com

KOREA:
Coats Korea Co Ltd
5F Kuckdong B/D
935-40 Bangbae- Dong
Seocho-Gu, Seoul
Tel: (82) 2 521 6262
Fax: (82) 2 521 5181

NEW ZEALAND
Individual stockists please contact
Rowan for details

NORWAY:
Coats Norge A/S
Postboks 63, 2801 Gjovik
Tel: (47) 61 18 34 00
Fax: (47) 61 18 34 20

SINGAPORE:
Golden Dragon Store
101 Upper Cross Street #02-51
People's Park Centre
Singapore 058357
Tel: (65) 6 5358454
Email: gdscraft@hotmail.com

SOUTH AFRICA:
Arthur Bales PTY
PO Box 44644
Linden 2104
Tel: ( 27 ) 11 888 2401

SPAIN:
Oyambre
Pau Claris 145, 80009 Barcelona
Tel: (34) 670 011957
Email:
comercial@oyambreonline.com

SWEDEN:
Wincent
Norrtullsgatan 65, 113 45
Stockholm
Tel: (46) 8 33 70 60
Fax: (46) 8 33 70 68
Email: wincent@chello.se
www.wincentyarn.com

TAIWAN :
Laiter Wool Knitting Co Ltd
10-1 313 Lane, Sec 3
Chung Ching North Road
Taipei
Tel: ( 886 ) 2 2596 0269

Long T eh Trading Co Ltd
3F No. 19-2
Kung Yuan Road, Taichung
Tel: (886) 4 2225 6698

Green Leave Thread Company
No 181
Sec 4 Chung Ching North Road
Taipei
Fax: (886) 2 8221 2919

U.S.A.:
Westminster Fibers Inc
4 Townsend West
Suite 8, Nashua
New Hampshire 03063
Tel: (1 603) 886 5041 / 5043
Email:
rowan@westminsterfibers.com

U.K.:
Rowan Yarns
Green Lane Mill, Holmfirth
West Yorkshire, HD9 2DX.
Tel : 01484 681881
Email: bigitup@knitrowan.com.
www.knitrowan.com

For all other countries:
please contact Rowan for
stockist details.

For details of U.K. stockists or any
other information concerning this
brochure please contact:
Rowan Yarns, Green Lane Mill,
Holmfirth, West Yorkshire,
England, HD9 2DX
Email: bigitup@knitrowan.com
Internet: www.knitrowan.com

# INFORMATION

## TENSION

Obtaining the correct tension is perhaps the single factor which can make the difference between a successful garment and a disastrous one. It controls both the shape and size of an article, so any variation, however slight, can distort the finished garment.

Different designers feature in our books and it is **their** tension, given at the **start** of each pattern, which you must match. We recommend that you knit a square in pattern and/or stocking stitch (depending on the pattern instructions) of perhaps 5 - 10 more stitches and 5 - 10 more rows than those given in the tension note. Mark out the central 10cm square with pins. If you have too many stitches to 10cm try again using thicker needles, if you have too few stitches to 10cm try again using finer needles. Once you have achieved the correct tension your garment will be knitted to the measurements indicated in the size diagram shown at the end of the pattern.

## SIZING & SIZE DIAGRAM NOTE

The instructions are given for the smallest size. Where they vary, work the figures in brackets for the larger sizes. **One set of figures refers to all sizes.** Included with most patterns in this brochure is a 'size diagram', or sketch of the finished garment and its dimensions. The size diagram shows the finished width of the garment at the under-arm point, and it is this measurement that the knitter should choose first; a useful tip is to measure one of your own garments which is a comfortable fit. Having chosen a size based on width, look at the corresponding length for that size; if you are not happy with the total length which we recommend, adjust your own garment before beginning your armhole shaping - any adjustment after this point will mean that your sleeve will not fit into your garment easily - don't forget to take your adjustment into account if there is any side seam shaping. Finally, look at the sleeve length; the size diagram shows the finished sleeve measurement, taking into account any top-arm insertion length. Measure your body between the centre of your neck and your wrist, this measurement should correspond to half the garment width plus the sleeve length. Again, your sleeve length may be adjusted, but remember to take into consideration your sleeve increases if you do adjust the length - you must increase more frequently than the pattern states to shorten your sleeve, less frequently to lengthen it.

## CHART NOTE

Many of the patterns in the brochure are worked from charts. Each square on a chart represents a stitch and each line of squares a row of knitting. Each colour used is given a different letter and these are shown in the **materials** section, or in the **key** alongside the chart of each pattern. When working from the charts, read odd rows (K) from right to left and even rows (P) from left to right, unless otherwise stated.

## KNITTING WITH COLOUR

There are two main methods of working colour into a knitted fabric: **Intarsia** and **Fairisle** techniques. The first method produces a single thickness of fabric and is usually used where a colour is only required in a particular area of a row and does not form a repeating pattern across the row, as in the fairisle technique.
**Intarsia:** The simplest way to do this is to cut short lengths of yarn for each motif or block of colour used in a row. Then joining in the various colours at the appropriate point on the row, link one colour to the next by twisting them around each other where they meet on the wrong side to avoid gaps. All ends can then either be darned along the colour join lines, as each motif is completed or then can be " knitted-in" to the fabric of the knitting as each colour is worked into the pattern. This is done in much the same way as "weaving- in" yarns when working the Fairisle technique and does save time darning-in ends. It is essential that the tension is noted for **Intarsia** as this may vary from the stocking stitch if both are used in the same pattern.
**Fairisle type knitting:** When two or three colours are worked repeatedly across a row, strand the yarn **not** in use loosely behind the stitches being worked. If you are working with more than two colours, treat the "floating" yarns as if they were one yarn and always spread the stitches to their correct width to keep them elastic. It is advisable not to carry the stranded or "floating" yarns over more than three stitches at a time, but to weave them under and over the colour you are working. The "floating" yarns are therefore caught at the back of the work.

## CROCHET TERMS

UK crochet terms and abbreviations have been used throughout. The list below gives the US equivalent where they vary.

| Abbreviation | UK | US |
|---|---|---|
| **dc** | double crochet | single crochet |

## FINISHING INSTRUCTIONS

After working for hours knitting a garment, it seems a great pity that many garments are spoiled because such little care is taken in the pressing and finishing process. Follow the following tips for a truly professional-looking garment.

## PRESSING

Block out each piece of knitting and following the instructions on the ball band press the garment pieces, omitting the ribs. Tip: Take special care to press the edges, as this will make sewing up both easier and neater. If the ball band indicates that the fabric is not to be pressed, then covering the blocked out fabric with a damp white cotton cloth and leaving it to stand will have the desired effect. Darn in all ends neatly along the selvage edge or a colour join, as appropriate.

## STITCHING

When stitching the pieces together, remember to match areas of colour and texture very carefully where they meet. Use a seam stitch such as back stitch or mattress stitch for all main knitting seams and join all ribs and neckband with mattress stitch, unless otherwise stated.

## CONSTRUCTION

Having completed the pattern instructions, join left shoulder and neckband seams as detailed above. Sew the top of the sleeve to the body of the garment using the method detailed in the pattern, referring to the appropriate guide:
**Shallow set–in sleeves:** Match decreases at beg of armhole shaping to decreases at top of sleeve. Sew sleeve head into armhole, easing in shapings.
**Set– in sleeves:** Place centre of cast-off edge of sleeve to shoulder seam. Set in sleeve, easing sleeve head into armhole.

Join side and sleeve seams.
Slip stitch pocket edgings and linings into place.
Sew on buttons to correspond with buttonholes.
Ribbed welts and neckbands and any areas of garter stitch should not be pressed.

## EXPERIENCE RATINGS & ABBREVIATIONS

Easy, straight forward knitting / crocheting

Suitable for the average knitter / crocheter

For the more experienced knitter / crocheter

| | | | |
|---|---|---|---|
| **K** | knit | **rep** | repeat |
| **P** | purl | **alt** | alternate |
| **st(s)** | stitch(es) | **cont** | continue |
| **inc** | increas(e)(ing) | **patt** | pattern |
| **dec** | decreas(e)(ing) | **tog** | together |
| **st st** | stocking stitch (1 row K, 1 row P) | **mm** | millimetres |
| **g st** | garter stitch (K every row) | **cm** | centimetres |
| **beg** | begin(ning) | **in(s)** | inch(es) |
| **foll** | following | **RS** | right side |
| **rem** | remain(ing) | **WS** | wrong side |
| **rev st st** | reverse stocking stitch (1 row P, 1 row K) | **sl 1** | slip one stitch |
| | | **psso** | pass slipped stitch over |

| | |
|---|---|
| **tbl** | through back of loop |
| **M1P** | make one stitch by picking up horizontal loop before next stitch and purling into back of it |
| **yfwd** | yarn forward |
| **meas** | measures |
| **0** | no stitches, times or rows |
| **-** | no stitches, times or rows for that size |
| **approx** | approximately |

Photographer Joey Toller • Stylist Harris Elliott • Hair & Make-up KJ • Model Kiera Gormly
Design Layout Simon Wagstaff

First published in Great Britain in 2005 by Rowan Yarns Ltd, Green Lane Mill, Holmfirth, West Yorkshire, England, HD9 2DX
Internet: www.knitrowan.com Email: bigitup@knitrowan.com
© Copyright Rowan 2005
British Library Cataloguing in Publication Data Rowan Yarns - Big It Up
ISBN 1-904485-43-X